TERRY FOX

FOX

His Story

TERRY

NEW REVISED EDITION

FOX

His Story

LESLIE SCRIVENER

Copyright © 1981, 1983, 2000 by The Terry Fox Foundation

Original edition published 1981
Revised edition published 1983
New revised edition published 2000

Canadian Cataloguing in Publication Data

Scrivener, Leslie, 1950-
   Terry Fox: his story

New rev. ed.
ISBN 0-7710-8019-0

1. Fox, Terry, 1958-1981. 2. Cancer – Patients – Biography. 3. Runners (Sports) – Canada – Biography. I. Title.

RC263.S37 2000   362.1'96994'0092   C00-931194-7

We acknowledge the financial support of the Government of Canada through the Book Publishing Industry Development Program for our publishing activities. We further acknowledge the support of the Canada Council for the Arts and the Ontario Arts Council for our publishing program.

Map by VisuTronx
Typeset in Janson by M&S, Toronto
Printed and bound in Canada

McClelland & Stewart Ltd.
The Canadian Publishers
481 University Avenue
Toronto, Ontario
M5G 2E9
www.mcclelland.com

1 2 3 4 5   04 03 02 01 00

CONTENTS

For David

PREFACE TO THE NEW, REVISED EDITION

For many of us who were lucky enough to see Terry Fox run across Canada in the summer of 1980, it seems impossible that twenty years have passed. Terry remains forever young – caught in those summer days of courage and joy and heartbreak. Yet much has changed as not only Canadians but people around the world have caught on to Terry's dream of finding a cure for cancer.

The first edition of *Terry Fox: His Story* was written while Terry was still alive. This new edition, which commemorates the twentieth anniversary of his Marathon of Hope, brings us up to date on Terry's legacy – the $250 million raised in his name, the stories of men, women, and children who work in his memory, and the scientists whose research is made possible through Terry Fox grants. There is also the greater gift of his example of hope, which we saw pounded out on Canada's highways. Darrell Fox asked me to revisit Terry's story, and I thank him for this chance to think and write about Terry once again.

I would never have guessed how deeply Terry affected many people and how alive and real he became to those who never knew him until I talked to those people myself. It's been a joy and a privilege.

I have run the great race
I have finished the course
I have kept faith
And now the prize awaits me

2 Timothy 4:7-8

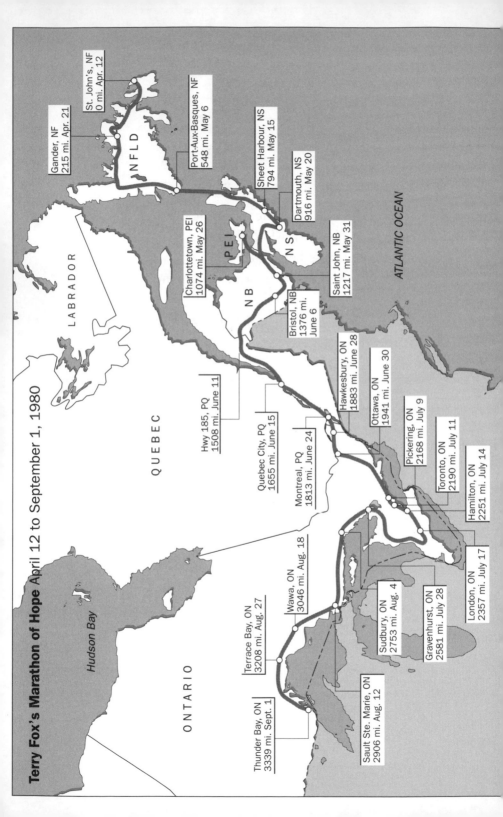

Terry Fox's Marathon of Hope April 12 to September 1, 1980

LABRADOR

QUEBEC

ONTARIO

N F L D

P E I

N B

N S

ATLANTIC OCEAN

Hudson Bay

St. John's, NF
0 mi. Apr. 12

Gander, NF
215 mi. Apr. 21

Port-Aux-Basques, NF
548 mi. May 6

Sheet Harbour, NS
794 mi. May 15

Dartmouth, NS
916 mi. May 20

Charlottetown, PEI
1074 mi. May 26

Saint John, NB
1217 mi. May 31

Bristol, NB
1376 mi.
June 6

Hwy 185, PQ
1508 mi. June 11

Quebec City, PQ
1655 mi. June 15

Montreal, PQ
1813 mi. June 24

Hawkesbury, ON
1883 mi. June 28

Ottawa, ON
1941 mi. June 30

Pickering, ON
2168 mi. July 9

Toronto, ON
2190 mi. July 11

Hamilton, ON
2251 mi. July 14

London, ON
2357 mi. July 17

Gravenhurst, ON
2581 mi. July 28

Sudbury, ON
2753 mi. Aug. 4

Sault Ste. Marie, ON
2906 mi. Aug. 12

Wawa, ON
3046 mi. Aug. 18

Terrace Bay, ON
3208 mi. Aug. 27

Thunder Bay, ON
3339 mi. Sept. 1

"THE WHOLE THING WAS

SUCH AN ADVENTURE"

"The whole thing was such an adventure and all of it was happening to me. People began calling me a hero, but as far as I was concerned, I was just simple little old Terry Fox. I was like Dorothy in *The Wizard of Oz*, going through this great big adventure, going places she had never been and seeing things she had never seen before and things happening that had never happened.

"I loved it. I enjoyed myself so much and that was what other people couldn't realize. They thought I was going through a nightmare running all day long. People thought I was going through hell. Maybe I was, partly, but still I was doing what I wanted and a dream was coming true and that, above everything else, made it all worthwhile to me. Even though it was so difficult, there was not another thing in the world I would rather have been doing.

"I got satisfaction out of doing things that were difficult. It was an incredible feeling. The pain was there, but the pain didn't matter. But that's all a lot of people could see; they couldn't see the good that I was getting out of it myself."

"IF IT'S ONLY UP TO ME"

On April 12, 1980, Terry Fox stood with his back to the sea, his arms behind him and his eyes straight ahead, his mind fixed on a distant shore. All of Canada – 5,300 miles, ten provinces – stretched as in a dream before him, and in a moment he would take his first steps towards that dream. He was going to run across Canada.

They knew something of dreamers in St. John's, Newfoundland. Canada's most easterly city, set on rock above the Atlantic Ocean, was either the beginning or the end for cross-country travellers. It seemed as often as once a week, a young man like Terry, strong and full of purpose, wanted to run or cycle across Canada for a cause he believed in. Some hoped for a little more attention. Some they never heard from again. On this bitterly cold, rainy morning – winter was still abounding, as they put it – they were preparing another goodbye and good-luck ceremony.

Terry was more interesting than many. He had sponsors, he had the support of the Canadian Cancer Society, he had

Canada's national broadcaster, the CBC, preparing to record his start, he had a handsome face, perfect teeth, and curly hair. And he had only one leg. His right leg was a stump, amputated six inches above the knee, and attached to it was a prosthesis, an artificial leg consisting of a fibreglass bucket with a steel shank. His left leg was taut and muscular.

He'd started his day at the Holiday Inn. He pulled on a pair of jeans and a ski jacket and went downstairs for breakfast. The hotel was looking after his meals and room while he was in St. John's, and that made him happy. It was a sign that people were taking him and his dream – he called his journey a Marathon of Hope – seriously. It could have been a bad joke. After all, a one-legged runner who dreamed of crossing Canada? Most cross-country runners preferred to start in Vancouver and take advantage of the westerly winds. These runs often ended in Halifax, Nova Scotia, a journey nine hundred miles shorter than the one Terry planned.

He ordered a meal loaded with carbohydrates. He didn't care if he was teased about his appetite. Let them laugh at his French toast, hash browns, and muffins. He knew they were foods that gave him energy; the calories served their purpose.

With Terry was his old school friend and fellow athlete, Doug Alward. Shy, soft-spoken, patient, and loyal, Doug was twenty-one, the same age as Terry. He was slightly built, with dark, thinning hair and glasses. Together they left the hotel to look at their brand-new camper van, donated by Ford of Canada and outfitted by Funcraft. It had air conditioning, a stove, a fridge, a washroom, a stereo, and it could sleep six. On the side was printed MARATHON OF HOPE CROSS COUNTRY RUN IN AID OF CANCER RESEARCH. The inside was a disorganized muddle of groceries: boxes of cereal, oranges, chocolate chip cookies, bags of chips, boxes of doughnuts, tins of stew and spaghetti, peanut butter and jelly.

Later, Donna Green, a girl Terry had met at the New-foundland Summer Games, stopped by to give him a good-luck card and a pennant. Terry, who had wanted to collect mementos of his trip, thought that pennants from every town along the way would be a good way to remember his route. Back at the hotel, he took a nap until Bill Strong, field supervisor for the Canadian Cancer Society, stopped by to take him for a drive.

Strong remembered that Terry wanted to fill two one-gallon jugs with Atlantic seawater, which he planned to carry in the van until they reached the Pacific Ocean. He would empty one at the end of his run and keep the other as a souvenir. Strong thought Terry should have good fresh seawater as a remembrance of his journey, not the murky water below the city wharf.

They drove to the outskirts of St. John's, where the bald and rocky shore meets the sea. It was a grey day. The rain had stopped, but clouds and mist hugged the hills. The cove was deserted. Strong volunteered to fill the jugs because Terry couldn't move fast enough to avoid the waves. He perched on what seemed to be a safe rock when a cold wave of Atlantic sea-water crashed around him, soaking his three-piece suit. "I was distraught," Strong said. He was so distraught he dropped the gallon jug and watched miserably as it floated out to sea. Terry hooted with laughter and offered to try himself. Strong took photographs while Terry half-filled the jug and walked back up the shingle beach.

He had wanted to start his marathon at the ocean early in the morning, but organizers asked him to set out from City Hall later in the afternoon. His desire to run and get the miles behind him while accommodating officials and fundraising opportunities was a struggle from the first moments of the Marathon of Hope.

With a small group of runners and a CBC film crew, Terry did start at the ocean, at the foot of Temperance Street near the harbour. This time he wore shorts and a T-shirt. The beach was muddy, littered with construction debris for a sewage tunnel. There were bulldozers behind him and guy wires covered with seaweed. It was an ugly little place, Terry said, but it was the beginning.

CBC television cameras recorded the moment, Strong took photographs, sea gulls squawked, and Terry dipped his artificial leg in the water and bent down to touch the pebbles. In his mind, he had to touch something for the run to count. He set off up a gravel hill – too steep and slippery for running – with a handful of spectators beside him. He told reporters he wanted to raise one million dollars and hoped to run thirty to forty miles a day to get home to Port Coquitlam, near Vancouver, within six months. He even planned to run across Vancouver Island to Port Renfrew so he could dip his leg in the Pacific. His run, like Canada's motto, would be from sea to sea.

A reporter remarked that he sounded confident.

"If it's only up to me and my mind," Terry said, "I've got a lot of positive attitude. I think I can do it. But you never know what might happen."

He left the reporters behind and started running through the old, worn-down part of St. John's, past boarded-up shops and tumbledown marinas. Occasionally, people would turn to watch. You could see the impression he made: their expressions showed astonishment and then admiration. It was clear what they were thinking: He's running with only one leg. How can he do it?

People were cheering and clapping. This was new and exciting for Terry, who had trained alone and wasn't used to the attention. He thought to himself: "I'm not training, now. I'm running across the country. This mile counts."

He gave them a wave and continued up the broad ramp leading to St. John's showy, slate-grey city hall. Mayor Dorothy Wyatt herself welcomed him. She was wearing dark glasses and, beneath her robes of office, a startling polka-dot pant suit. She clasped Terry to her as though he were her son, dropped her chain of office over his T-shirt, and hung on his arm as he signed her guest book. The book rested on a wooden podium carved with the Lamb of St. John the Baptist. The room was fragrant with Easter lilies. Terry smiled as Strong took more photographs. The thought came to him again, "This is really it." Wyatt draped her red and gold robe over Terry's shoulders and led him out to the terrace to talk to the crowd outside. He worried that he looked foolish in his shorts with the gaudy chain around his neck and the long robe. Mayor Wyatt presented him with messages for the mayors of Vancouver and Victoria, and a little flag for him, which he twirled in his hand. She ordered that the Canadian Cancer Society flag be raised. In her speech to the crowd – they seemed chilly and kept their hands in their parka pockets – she spoke of the great challenge that lay before Terry. Then he made his first speech. He said how he had lost his leg to cancer and he challenged the people of Newfoundland to match his running effort by donating money.

Wyatt took the stand again and again ordered that the Cancer Society flag be raised. It was already up. Terry grinned. The crowd laughed. The irrepressible mayor grinned. Terry returned her robe and chain, turned around, waved goodbye, and was off.

He started running, taking a double hop with the left leg and one long step with his metal leg. Someone called it the Fox Trot. His hands were clenched. He leaned forward for more speed. Looks of disbelief crossed the faces of the hundred or so onlookers. Then they gave a cheer and clapped. A police cruiser, its lights flashing, drove beside Terry. Wyatt set off enthusiastically behind, her robe flapping. She couldn't keep up. Terry ran out on the highway past the hills dotted with patches of snow. The fishing boats and wharves were far behind, but the mayor wasn't. She caught up in her car, took off her red robe, and skipped

along behind him, her chain of office beating on her pant suit as
she ran. It was wacky and wonderful and Terry was delighted.
He'd never forget any of it.

A mile or so out of St. John's, Terry felt his sock was wet and
stopped to ask Doug to find a dry one. It was mid-afternoon and
Terry was anxious to get the miles behind him.

Doug hadn't had time to get the van in order and it was difficult to find a sock quickly beneath the bags of groceries. Terry
was impatient. After the excitement of the ceremonies and
wishes for his success, it seemed absurd for him to stand on the
highway waiting for Doug to get a dry sock.

"I could tell," Doug said mournfully, "that our troubles had
already started."

All that afternoon, passing drivers honked their horns and
waved to him. Terry loved it. Doug kept the van in front of him,
driving one mile ahead and waiting until Terry caught up.
Terry's thoughts also ran ahead. He imagined the road would be
lonely for the next six months, but he was used to running alone.
He thought about Stanley Park in Vancouver, the end of his
journey. He'd be the happiest man in Canada. He felt the cold.
He was used to that, too. He could run in rain and bitter wind,
he could run uphill and down, he could run a hundred days in a
row without taking a break. He'd become strong and used to
pain. He could run under any conditions. His inner strength
matched the strength of his body.

Terry wasn't troubled by self-doubt or depression; on the
contrary, he was brimming with determination and hope. He
was a dreamer, although the immensity of his vision never
daunted him, even as he pounded out those first miles. "Who
would have thought it would be possible to run across Canada
on one leg, eh?" he said. "I wanted to try the impossible and
show that it could be done. I've always been competitive and I

wanted to show myself, and other people, too, that I could do it. To show them that I wasn't disabled or handicapped."

That was only part of the reason he was running. He wanted to talk about cancer. He wanted everyone to believe, as he did, that the disease that killed thousands of Canadians every year could be beaten. After all, he'd lost a leg to cancer, and here he was running across Canada.

Terry saw himself as an ordinary person, average in every-thing but his determination. His tastes were simple. He loved sports, and admired two hockey stars in particular, Bobby Orr and Darryl Sittler. He was close to his family. He appreciated pretty girls and enjoyed inspirational poetry. He was a loyal friend. He worked hard for everything he achieved. He was touched by the spontaneity of small children. He believed in national unity, and was puzzled by the efforts of the province of Quebec to separate from the rest of Canada.

He ran twelve and a half miles that first day. They had been invited back to the Holiday Inn in St. John's to sleep. Terry was accustomed to sleeping in the van but the van's propane heater wasn't working and they knew it would be a cold night. In his room, Terry took out his diary, a big ledger-sized book, and wrote: "Today is the day it all begins." He filled a page, then fell asleep, contented.

As he slept, his parents were awake on the other side of the country, tuned to the CBC national news, amazed to see the beginning of Terry's dream broadcast across the land.

The next day Terry began to understand the audacity of that dream and the punishing price of achievement. He started running at 4:30 a.m. Later in the day he was buffeted by forty-mile-an-hour winds, which tore through his light jacket and three layers of shirts. He told his diary, "It knocked me off the road and almost on my butt." The sores on his stump started hurting. His heart began to flutter dangerously. He rested, wrapped in a blanket. By mid-afternoon, he had run twenty miles. It was the toughest twenty miles he had ever run but, always striving to do better, he told himself if not for the vicious wind that blew across the frozen lakes onto the highway, he'd have run thirty miles.

When Terry turned off the light in the lower bunk of the van that night, he thought the next day might be worse. The forecast called for snow. By breakfast he was running in a blizzard and slipping on the icy road; by lunch the wind held him to a standstill. Yet by the end of the day he'd run sixteen miles. That night, they parked the van in a schoolyard. They would search out quiet places, sometimes even cemeteries, to rest. Sometime in the night, a Royal Canadian Mounted Police constable knocked on the door of the van and offered them a motel room.

The next day Doug started accepting donations through the van window as he waited for Terry at each mile marker. One driver pulled up and pushed fifty dollars through the window. "I don't care if he makes it," he told Doug. "He's really making a lot of people feel good."

They stopped that night at a store in Bellevue and were invited in by the Brazil family for a shower and a meal. Doug noticed that someone had clipped Terry's picture out of a newspaper and pinned it above the dining-room table.

Terry treasured every memory. Every cheer – the one he heard most often was pure Newfoundland: "You sure got the nerve" – every kind word, every offer of a meal helped him run another mile, helped ease the aches and the irritations and convinced him his dream was not foolish. Ordinary Canadians in those tiny seaside towns cared about him. He felt it. His hopes soared.

People heard his message: a disability didn't have to be a handicap. Cancer could be beaten. As the dollars poured in the van window, Terry, to his surprise, saw that he was inspiring others while being inspired himself.

"Knowing that there are people who care about what I'm doing, that I'm not just running across Canada, that there are people who are giving money to help fight the disease that took my leg and to help other people who are lying down in hospital beds all over the world. It was a great reward for me, the responses of the people and the way they've accepted what I've done. They could have written me off as a goof, running across Canada on one leg."

$$3$$

"THE LITTLE GUY WHO

WORKED HIS REAR OFF"

Terry's parents were Betty and Rolly Fox. When he started his run, Betty was forty-two. She had prematurely grey hair, which framed her head in tight curls. Her smile was pretty, and when it flashed you knew it was genuine. When she was angry, it was better to be out of the room. She was blunt, some might think to the point of harshness, and she was fiercely protective of her children, especially Terry. Her emotions were close to the surface; she could be moved to tears quickly.

Terry respected her judgement and agreed with most of her decisions. When he was running, many businessmen asked if Terry would endorse their product – one even said all Terry had to do was drive away in his company's car at the end of the run. They said no to every endorsement, to every offer of a donation that had some strings attached. Every cent was to go to cancer research. That was Terry's intention from the beginning of his run and it would continue forever after. If you give, your gift is pure charity, a gift from the heart, not one that benefits a company. No one was to profit from Terry's run, ever.

That's why his family appreciated Ford's donation of the camper van. The company offered the van two weeks after receiving a letter from Terry. "They didn't ask what kind of person he was. They trusted him from the beginning," Betty said.

His mother handled all such requests and, in Terry's eyes, she did a good job. It was as though they had one mind. She was proud to say, as she often did, "I know Terry better than anyone." In time, when reporters as well as curious or well-meaning people pried too much into their lives, she became even more vigilant and protective. It didn't matter what anyone thought or said; she was doing what was best for Terry.

Rolly was forty-five when Terry started running. He was a Canadian National Railway switchman, and had been since 1954. His hair was reddish brown, his complexion ruddy, and his temperament, to those who knew him a little, seemed quiet, though his family said he harboured a quick and stubborn temper. He had a generous nature and, though reticent, he warmed to strangers more quickly than Betty and always made an effort to make them feel at ease. It may have seemed he deferred to his wife, who eventually became the one who spoke on behalf of the family, but they were a team and made all decisions together.

They were down-to-earth, solid, and dependable. Nothing in the world was more important than their family. Their children were close to them without being dependent. It was a fine line, and they walked it expertly. They didn't go in for frills – both wore jeans as much as anything else – and they lived in a comfortable suburban home about seventeen miles east of Vancouver. In the living room there was a pair of carved moose on the mantel, and the fancy velvet pillows were kept under plastic. When they finished their basement, they put in a pool table.

Betty and Rolly met in Winnipeg. Betty had been a tomboy who could throw a ball with the best of her brothers. She left high school early to escape the little farming town of Melita to study hairdressing in the city. They married in 1956. She was a practical woman. When labour pains started with her first child and no one could drive her to the hospital, she simply packed her bags and walked.

Their first son, born in 1957, was named Fred, after her brother. The family would know tragedy when the elder Fred lost both his legs in a plane crash during a whiteout in northern Manitoba. A few years later, Betty's youngest sister, Norma, who lived with them, was killed when her car skidded into a tanker truck on black ice on the Lougheed Highway. The family wondered if somehow they had been singled out for misfortune.

Terrance Stanley was born July 28, 1958, in Winnipeg, and was named after uncles on both sides of the family. Darrell was born in 1962, followed three years later by Judith. The family was complete.

Early pictures show Terry as a serious child, wearing a white shirt and bow tie in one photo, a cowboy shirt with fringed trousers in another. Even as a child, the qualities that would bring him success in later life were in place. He was determined and tenacious. Betty recalled that as a toddler he stacked wooden blocks tirelessly. If they tumbled down, he'd try again and again until they stayed in place.

That stubborn streak was a family trait. When Betty gave up smoking her friends told her she'd start again. The taunt was a challenge. She never gave anyone the satisfaction of saying, "I told you so."

Terry developed patience, too. As a child he loved games that lasted a long time. Luckily, he enjoyed his own company because few children had his perseverance even in play. He could amuse himself for hours. Sometimes he set up a table-hockey game and devised a long, complicated season's schedule. He would play for both teams, allowing three passes before he would switch sides and shoot for the other team. He continued playing long after his interest in working the players had waned, he said, because he wanted to see who won. Also, as his father had taught him, he liked to finish what he started.

Terry loved playing with toy soldiers, too. He would bundle up carpets and make fortresses of them in the basement, arranging his armies of cowboys and Indians or soldiers from both world wars on either side. When the soldiers lay face down, they were dead; face up, they were wounded. He fought to the last man.

Betty and Rolly were close to their brothers and sisters and the couples, with their growing families, often spent time together. At one family picnic, when the children were playing softball, Terry's nose started bleeding. It bled so much he had to be taken to a hospital where the flow was stemmed by cauterization. But Terry was back in no time, ready to rejoin his cousins and play ball. The adults were surprised, except his parents, who shrugged it off. That was Terry.

By 1966 Rolly wanted a change from the harsh Manitoba winters. He transferred to Vancouver, B.C., and lost twelve years' seniority. Two years later, he moved the family to Port Coquitlam.

The boys all loved sports, whether it was road hockey or baseball, and they all liked to win, no matter what they were playing. Sometimes Terry and Fred would gang up on Rolly as he lay on the chesterfield. They would pummel him, and he'd fight them both. Each one did his best to get in the last punch, although Fred and Terry would usually be in tears before the rough-housing was over. "We really fought dirty," Terry remembered. "We'd be bawling our eyes out but we'd come back for more. Even to get one more shot in was worth it."

Since Rolly frequently worked the afternoon shift, it was often Betty who threw a ball in the backyard with her sons. When Terry learned how to throw a baseball, Betty played catcher.

After Rolly got off shift, they would watch their sons compete in soccer games. Often all three boys were playing in different age groups on three different soccer fields in the same day.

Discipline in the Fox household was strict. Rolly tended to be hotheaded but quick to forgive. He might hastily send a child to his room before he heard the child's side of the story, but he might just as quickly say he was sorry and set the child free. When Betty sent the children to their rooms, they stayed.

Betty and Rolly insisted on good behaviour and respect for older people. Well into adulthood, the Fox children would continue to address family friends as Mr., Mrs., or Miss. They changed their clothes after school before going out to play. Good table manners were important, too: use your knife and fork, keep elbows off the table, no hats at the table.

They were expected to stay out of trouble, and if they got a job, they were to keep it. The children started berry-picking when they were nine or ten years old and continued at these seasonal jobs when they were teenagers. By twelve or thirteen, they were buying their own school clothes and later would buy their own golf clubs and ten-speed bikes. "Everything wasn't handed to them, they all had to learn to do for themselves," Betty said. The children didn't have paper routes because she said it wasn't fair to make them get up at 5:00 a.m. They needed rest and they needed time to play.

Terry was enthusiastic about sports and worked hard in every game. In elementary school, he played baseball. Sometimes he'd arrive an hour early at the corner where he was to pick up his ride, just to make sure he'd get to the park on time. He'd kick the curb for a half-hour, then he'd worry that he was late and had missed the ride until the driver turned up at the right time.

When they were in grade eight, Bob McGill, the physical-education teacher at Mary Hill Junior High School, noticed two young players: Terry and his friend Doug Alward. Terry was "the little guy who worked his rear off. If there was a race, he'd be in the middle of the pack. In class, he'd be sitting three-quarters of the way back, so small that in the big junior-high desks his feet wouldn't touch the floor. His head would be lowered, and if a teacher was looking for answers to questions, Terry would be saying to himself, 'Oh, God, please don't let him ask me, please. If he does, I'll just die.' And if a girl happened to look his way, he'd just shy away."

Doug was much the same. He and Terry had at least three things in common in grade eight: both were introverts, both stood five feet tall, and both were crazy for basketball. Doug, who was also a talented cross-country runner, was a first-string basketball player; Terry, however, was terrible at the game, even by the standards of the Mary Hill Cobras.

McGill suggested Terry try out for cross-country running. He might as well have asked Terry to skydive. The boy had no interest in running, but Terry started training anyway, because he had so much respect for the coach and wanted to please him. He found the workouts exhausting, and was often afraid to start the runs because they were so demanding. The biggest reward came at the end, when the coach would welcome the runners in, and say, "Well done, men." That's what Terry remembered: his teacher congratulating the skinny boys by calling them men.

Terry still wanted to play basketball. After three basketball practices, McGill suggested that he might be better suited for wrestling. There were other small boys who showed more ability than Terry as guards. But Terry was determined to stick with the game, even if he was the nineteenth player on a team of nineteen. He worked hard in practice and was rewarded with one minute of floor play all season. He thought his teammates laughed at him for that, but he didn't let it get him down.

That summer he called Doug and said, "Do you want to play a little one-on-one?" Doug, at the other end of the line, paused, remembering that Terry was a pretty fair runner, but a lousy basketball player, and said no. But Terry persisted. The second time he called, Doug agreed. "I could probably beat him twenty-one to nothing, but I don't remember if I ever did. He might get ten points off me," Doug said, "but the point was he couldn't beat me."

The two boys played hard all summer. Doug's older brother Jack, who was a gifted high-school basketball player, often joined them. By grade nine, there were four boys pounding the floor of the Mary Hill gym every morning before school. Doug wasn't one of them, but Terry was.

"Mom and Dad didn't like me getting up early to go to school to play basketball," Terry recalled. "Because they didn't want me to go early, I'd wait until the very last minute to get out of bed. I'd eat my breakfast as fast as I could, and I'd run all the way – and Mary Hill was far from our house. I'd run in the dark with all my books and clothes flying."

He remembered days when he felt sick with flu or a cold, when he should have stayed in bed, but he forced himself to his feet and ran to school anyway. He didn't want to fall behind in his classwork, but most of all he didn't want to miss a moment of basketball. Bob McGill had that effect on all the boys on the team. When he said, "If you want something, you work for it, because I'm not interested in mediocrity," Terry and the others listened. McGill told them they could be the best, but only if they got up early, practised before school, and stayed late afterwards. Terry responded to his teacher's challenge. He didn't call him Mr. McGill as the other boys did. He called him Coach, and said it with respect.

McGill's policy was not to cut anyone from the team, but he let the boys know that only the twelve best players would be allowed floor time. In grade nine, Terry was one of the twelve best. He wanted to be as good as the coach believed he could be. "He was such an inspirational person, I wanted to show him that I was a lot better than being laughed at by the other players," Terry recalled.

McGill chuckled with pride, remembering the way he pushed and encouraged the team, and the way Terry, in particular, responded: "If I had told Terry to hit his head against the wall, he would have," McGill said, "because that's how much he believed in what I was trying to do."

By grade ten, Terry had earned a place on the team as a starting guard. His pal Doug was a co-winner of the Athlete of the Year Award at Mary Hill. They'd both earned respect. McGill remembered Doug and Terry as starting guards in a game against the team with the tallest players in the league. When the Johnston Heights boys lined up against the Mary Hill boys, they just started laughing. Doug and Terry were now both five-foot-six, but the boys they had to check seemed like giants. There's no question which team won, but at the end of the game, the two Johnston Heights guards came over to shake hands with Doug and Terry. They knew they'd been in a game.

In grade eleven, when Terry joined the Port Coquitlam High School Ravens basketball team, he was a starting guard. Doug, who had taken a term at Centennial High School because it offered a better athletic program, remembered Terry once scored twenty points in the first half of a game. "All of a sudden, he'd become somebody by working hard," Doug said. Even when the team was being clobbered, the basketball coach, Terri Fleming, recalled that Terry never gave up.

By 1976, the one-on-one games between Terry and Doug were repeated, but with a twist: Terry could now beat Doug twenty-one to nothing. Except once. Doug recalled: "Terry was taller than me in grade twelve, and I remember playing with him in practice. I faked him out and, to my horror, I scored on him. I couldn't believe I had scored. He was mad, and the reason he was mad was that he had let down. He had thought, 'Ah, Alward, I can stuff him,' but I had faked him out. He picked up the basketball and slammed it down hard on the floor. The other guys in the line-up just looked on in stunned silence."

Terry shared the Athlete of the Year Award with Doug in grade twelve. Doug had become an accomplished runner and came second in the British Columbia cross-country finals. He always liked to deflect attention from himself, saying that Terry deserved the award more than he did because Terry was a better basketball player, a first-class soccer player, and a gutsy rugby player. Doug recalled one rugby game in particular: "This big guy got by everybody, and Terry was the last guy to stop him. Terry got him with this fantastic tackle. Man, he was tough! I could feel it from the sidelines. Holy cow, he should have had pads on. He may have been scared, but he'd stand there and face it."

Later, when Doug won a two-thousand-dollar Nancy Greene Scholarship to university, he wrote a cheque for that amount and sent it to Terry with a note saying Terry was a better athlete and more deserving of the award. Terry returned the cheque, but no one forgot Doug's kindness.

Although Terry remembers being an average student at Mary Hill, the truth is he and Doug made it to the honour roll a few times. Both had a fondness for biology. That science was made for them because it required lots of memorization. The two hard-driving athletes, who were by this time used to putting in long hours in training, applied the same discipline to memorizing a hundred pages of biology notes.

The competitive spirit they shared in sports was also apparent in their academic work. Doug, who seems to have been the sly one, turned to subterfuge to set Terry up again. This time his ploy was to tell Terry that he was not going to open a book to study for their next exam, but secretly, at home on the other side of town, Doug drove himself to desperation with study. When the exam results were posted, Terry was amazed to see that Doug had earned one of the top scores.

Later, analysing the outcomes, Doug thought he beat Terry – who, he believed, was more naturally gifted – because Terry let down his guard. In his mind the challenge was diminished. Why did Doug go through this exercise? "I wanted to beat him." Terry worked and played in a competitive world.

Betty was annoyed when Terry belittled his academic abilities. She wasn't a pushy mother, but she let him know she had high expectations of him. Terry remembered presenting his mother with his school report card and watching her carefully, wondering what she thought of his grades. Were they good enough? Was she proud of him? Was he doing well? "Sometimes, because I knew she cared, I'd do things for her," he said. "Even in school I wanted to get good grades to show her I could do it."

Terry's interests and friendships broadened in high school, and he and Doug drifted apart. Terry spent more time with his basketball teammates. He went to parties with them, would have a few drinks, and remembered getting roaring drunk a couple of times. He even dated occasionally. "There were lots of girls I knew who liked me and wanted to go out with me, but I was still too shy," he said. He didn't have a steady girlfriend. He felt more at ease with his locker-room friends, and more than anything, he said, he enjoyed playing basketball. Terry wasn't interested in the drug culture that left some in his generation dozing on the beaches. He never sampled marijuana, not even out of curiosity.

Judith saw her older brother as a complex person. He was obedient – that wanting-to-please part of his personality – but Terry gave all of himself in everything he tried, and he expected the same from others. They would fight, she said, when she wouldn't do what her mother asked her to do. He was funny, too. He loved to joke around, wrestle, play hide-and-seek. "There was this silliness, all the time. He was an incredible person. He knew how to be serious and get the job done, but also had a lot of fun."

He graduated from Port Coquitlam High School with A's and one B. Memorization and all the self-discipline in the world couldn't get him through essay writing, the subtleties of *Waiting for Godot*, and other high-school literature assignments.

While Terry wasn't sure he wanted to go to university, Betty was sure that he should. He enrolled at Simon Fraser University in part to please her and in part for himself.

He knew he wanted to play more basketball, though he realized that the competition at university, especially at SFU, which had the best varsity team in British Columbia, would be fierce. Naturally, that would attract rather than deter Terry.

He was also thinking he might want to be a high-school physical-education teacher. He liked the idea of being "the coach" to a bunch of skinny boys with more drive than talent. Since he enjoyed sports he chose kinesiology, the study of human movement, as a major, although Betty would have preferred he enrol in one of the professions.

It didn't surprise any of his former coaches or friends that Terry tried out for the SFU junior varsity team. The two-week training camp run by basketball coach Alex Devlin was tough, more of an endurance test than anything else. Devlin and the players, including Mike McNeill, who later became the head basketball coach at SFU, saw others who were more gifted than Terry, but none showed more desire.

McNeill, a first-string guard on the varsity team, said: "In the summer after high school, we knew Terry was coming out for the team. I played against him offensively, and he wasn't that good, but defensively, he was one of the toughest I'd ever played against. He had a lot of pride and he worked hard."

During the training camp, Devlin told Terry, "We've been noticing you." His determination and hard work paid off. He made the team.

"There were more-talented players who didn't make it," McNeill recalled, "but Terry just out-gutted them. People tend to look in awe at players who have a lot of natural ability, but respect from other athletes goes to the guy who works really hard." That was Terry.

Terry believed the key to his success was his mental toughness. He had learned that training in junior high school as a cross-country runner, in the long hours playing one-on-one, and on the rugby field where his opponents would happily trample him into the mud. He had also learned it at home, where the friendly fisticuffs on the couch were replaced by lively, sometimes stormy, always stubborn debates over cards, over who was the best player in the National Hockey League, over anything. Terry liked to argue until his brother or father would give up, either from exhaustion or intimidation. In the Fox household, it seemed everybody shared that argumentative streak, the belief that you stick up for yourself, even if you are wrong. The habit of arguing reinforced his stubborn will.

4

"NOBODY IS EVER GOING
TO CALL ME A QUITTER"

O n November 12, 1976, Terry drove his 1968 green Cortina right into the back of a half-ton truck on the Lougheed Highway. He'd been dreamily watching construction of a new bridge over the Coquitlam River near the turnoff to his neighbourhood. Police arrived and Terry's car was towed away, never to be driven again. Terry walked away from the accident without a scratch. His right knee was a little sore, and he guessed he must have rammed it on the underside of the dashboard. He phoned his mother at the card shop where she worked, then hopped a bus to SFU and basketball practice.

In December, Terry noticed again a pain in that same knee. Many athletes have knee and ankle problems; aches are expected. Terry thought his ache was a result of playing so much basketball on the hard gym floor. He thought it might have been a cartilage problem, but whatever it was, he was going to ignore it until the end of the basketball season. He didn't mention it to his coach or his parents.

A week after the season ended, in the last week of February, Terry finally went to the university medical services and was told he had a chemical reaction – he was not told to what – in his knee and was given a handful of pills. He took the pills for five days and believed they had worked because he didn't feel the pain any more. He didn't know they were nothing more than painkillers.

One day at the beginning of March, Betty was home from work after an operation to remove a cyst from her foot. She looked out her living-room window and saw something terribly wrong. Terry, who had just run seven laps around the track at Hastings Junior High School, was limping slowly home. Betty slid down the front stairs to the door to help her son. She could barely stand up herself, but she grabbed him. The pain in his knee was unbearable.

She suggested a hot bath, the usual restorative, but rather than soothe his temper and pain, it exacerbated both. Terry could barely move and stumbled to bed.

The next day the knee was swollen and throbbing. Terry went to see a family doctor who was filling in for their own physician, Robert Heffelfinger. The doctor suspected that there was a serious problem, possibly even cancer, and referred Terry to a bone specialist. They weren't able to see a specialist immediately, so Betty lent Terry her crutches and Rolly drove him to the emergency room at the Royal Columbian Hospital in New Westminster. She waited by the phone.

Twenty minutes after Dr. Michael Piper, an orthopedic specialist on duty in the hospital's plaster room, saw Terry, he knew he wasn't dealing with water on the knee or a cartilage problem. After looking at the shadows on the X-rays, he suspected Terry had osteogenic sarcoma, a rare, malignant tumour that tends to develop more often in males than females and is most common among children and young adults aged ten to twenty-five. Sarcomas are tumours of the connective and supportive tissues of the body. Piper had seen only two tumours of that type in his practice.

Osteogenic sarcoma, although rare, is the most common primary cancer of the bone. It is a destroyer that usually begins its work near the knee and makes the bone soft and mushy so that the grain that streaks the bone looks like a highway that ends abruptly in a swamp. As the sarcoma grows, it breaks through the bone into surrounding muscles and tendons. Unlike lung cancer, which can be linked to environmental hazards such as smoking, no one knows what causes osteogenic sarcoma. Terry believed his car accident caused a weakness in his knee and made him susceptible to a tumour. His doctors said there was no connection.

Yet other pediatric oncologists say that it is not uncommon for osteosarcoma patients to report an earlier injury in the area where the tumour develops. Doctors still don't like to make the link between accidents and tumours, but generally, a typical osteosarcoma patient is an active, athletic, fast-growing young person. Many of them have had sports-related injuries.

There are factors in the body that stimulate the growth of various cells, and it's possible that during healing they turn on the wrong cells and stimulate the growth of a tumour instead.

Although the sarcoma was rare, people became more familiar with it after Edward Kennedy, Jr., son of the U.S. senator Ted Kennedy, lost his leg to the disease in 1973. He went on to become a disability-rights lawyer and advocate for the disabled.

If Piper's diagnosis was confirmed by further testing, including a bone scan, there was no time to delay. Terry would require immediate surgery. As soon as the malignant tumour develops, its cells start to multiply, and the body's immune systems cannot stand the attack by the aberrant cells. The tumour sends cells, like invasion forces, into the bloodstream to be carried all over the body.

Terry learned none of this that morning. The doctor took Rolly aside to say he believed Terry had a malignant tumour but he did not want the boy to be told until he had a second opinion. He suggested that Rolly take Terry out for breakfast and then bring him back to the hospital later, when a room would be available. In the meantime, Piper consulted with two senior surgeons and asked one of them if he would take the patient. Piper, who was orthopedic surgeon for the Vancouver Canucks hockey team, had been in practice three years and thought of orthopedics as a happy specialty, a practice of healing and mending, not of amputating. He would stay on the case, break the news to Terry, and perform the amputation.

Meanwhile, Rolly walked immediately to a phone booth to call Betty. As he was telling her the news, he broke down and cried. He knew he would have to face Terry a few minutes later, so he composed himself, struggled to remove the strain from his face, and took Terry to McDonald's. The bitterness Rolly still feels started growing that morning.

Terry was puzzled that day. He had been told nothing and couldn't understand why. If he had to go back to the hospital for more examinations – a bone scan, blood tests, a chest X-ray – it must be something serious; in fact, it might be something horrible. To him, horrible would have been a very bad cartilage or ligament problem.

While Terry had breakfast, a call was made to Judith Ray, head nurse on the children's orthopedic ward, to ask if she had room for an eighteen-year-old boy with possible osteogenic sarcoma. Would she accept him? She immediately said yes and told her staff. Several objected to an older patient, but Ray explained to them her feeling that the children's ward would be a better place for Terry. When a young person is sick, he needs to regress a little bit and become a little more of a child. She also thought seeing grievously ill patients on the adult ward would make his recovery more difficult.

"It's really hard when you're an older teenager and so many people are telling you to behave like a man, and you really wish you were just a kid again," said Ray.

After she greeted Terry, Rolly, and Betty, who had joined them, at the elevator, she asked him what he'd been told. He said his right knee hurt, and he was waiting for the results of tests. She could tell from the strain on his parents' faces they'd been told that Terry had cancer. She could tell by Terry's expression that he hadn't. Ray was disturbed. She couldn't understand why an eighteen-year-old hadn't been told he likely had cancer, while his parents already knew and were struggling to put on a brave face. She knew he had to be told as quickly as possible.

Terry was given a bed in a ward with eight other boys. Ray looked on it as a summer camp with children of all ages. She thought it would be good for Terry. It was more like a home than a hospital, and he might look on the younger boys as little brothers.

Besides, he was likely to find someone in worse condition than himself on the ward, and with so much activity there wasn't time for brooding or self-pity. Ray persuaded his parents that the ward was better for Terry than a private room.

On March 4, Ray took Terry for a bone scan, a test that would confirm the diagnosis. A technician gave him an injection of a radioactive material with an affinity for bone tissue, then looked at a screen to see where the substance localized. The tumour appeared as a hot spot on the screen. The diagnosis was immediately clear to the technician, and he made a sign to Ray – Terry had cancer.

On his way out in a wheelchair, Terry cheerfully said to the technician, "Thank you very much."

"Don't thank me," he replied.

"Why did he say that?" Terry asked Ray.

Thinking fast, she said, "Oh, most people don't thank you for sticking needles into them."

Since bad news wasn't delivered in a nine-bed ward, Betty, Rolly, Judith, and Darrell were taken with Terry into a little room near the admitting area. Betty caught Ray's eye, wondering if the younger children should listen. "You're all part of the family and you've got to share things," the nurse told them.

"I knew there was something wrong, oh boy, did I know," Terry remembered, "when the whole family came in and Mom put her arm around me. The doctor came in and just told me, 'You've got a malignant tumour.' I guess I was supposed to be upset but I didn't do anything. 'What's that?' I said."

Piper told him he had a type of cancer, that his leg would have to be amputated soon, that he would undergo a series of chemotherapy treatments because there might be cancer cells circulating in his blood, and that he was going to lose his hair. The doctor said that, because of advances in research, new drugs had been developed to give him a 50 per cent or more chance of survival. Two years earlier, his chances would have been about 15 per cent. From that moment, Terry believed in the value of cancer research.

The doctor also told Terry, because someone would eventually tell him, about a fifteen-year-old girl from Port Coquitlam who had gone to the same high school as Terry. She'd had the same type of tumour and had been cared for in the same ward. Terry asked what had happened to her. He was told she had died that summer.

Terry cursed and said, "I'm not ready to leave this world."

For a moment, Rolly forgot the ache in his heart and was completely surprised. He'd never heard Terry swear before.

Then came the tears. Terry dropped his head to his chest. His family went to him and they all wept together. Darrell, who was fifteen at the time, remembered he and little Judith "bawled our eyes out." Seeing how frightened and upset they were, Terry turned to comfort his younger brother and sister.

The Foxes may have been hard on one another, they may have been critical and competitive, but more than anything they were a close, strong family who had known tragedy and loss. They could handle this one, too. But Betty couldn't help wondering: Was there a God? She thought of the losses in their family over the years.

Doug Alward was there, too, waiting out in the hallway. Rolly called him in. "There was dead silence," he remembered. "It seemed as if no one knew what to say. I think Terry was crying and somehow I felt out of place."

After Piper left, Judith Ray dried her tears and set to work. "All right," she told Terry, "the news is crummy, but you can either mope or you can fight it." She suspected he was a fighter anyway. She told him many amputees played sports. Even now she was looking to the future, thinking about his healing.

When he asked her about university – he had six weeks left in his semester – she teased him, the beginning of a bantering rapport that would soon be established between them. "What are you trying to do? Get out of school? No way." She explained he could do his assignments with the help of a tutor while he learned to walk. Making arrangements with Simon Fraser University would give his parents something to do as well, and organizing Terry's classmates to tape his lectures would keep Doug busy.

After that night, Terry never looked back. His world was turned around, but he decided to look on the loss of his leg as a new challenge. He was going to work hard, just as he had worked hard for all of his accomplishments. He would apply his mental toughness to this new situation. He could be just as positive with one leg as he had been with two.

He didn't want any sympathy or pity. He wouldn't sulk or become depressed. He was so successful in thinking positively that when he had visitors he would cheer them up. They usually left feeling better than they had when they walked in.

Family, friends, his coaches, his basketball teammates came to visit. Classmates from university brought homework. These visits and the cards and letters that covered the bedside table were encouraging, and he never forgot any of it.

"All the support I had from other people really helped me," Terry said, "knowing that all those people cared. That and being really competitive. I decided I was going to beat it and get off my butt and show these people what I could do, and that I appreciated them coming to see me and that I was not all sad and gloomy. So I decided that I would do my very best, that I would try to recuperate as fast as I could."

Terri Fleming, his basketball coach at PoCo, was nervous about seeing Terry. He wondered what he could say to a young man who was going to have his leg amputated. Knowing Terry, he wanted to do something upbeat, so he found a recent issue of *Runner's World*, which included a story about an above-the-knee amputee, Dick Traum, who had run in the New York Marathon. The article didn't elicit any immediate reaction from Terry, but the coach hoped it would give the boy something to think about.

Terry did think about it. He thought, What if I could do something like that? What if I could run, maybe run across Canada? There was no plan yet – that would come two years later – but an idea was planted in his mind.

"It was an impossible dream, a fantasy. That's what it was," Terry recalled. "I was lying in bed looking at this magazine, thinking if he can do it, I can do it, too. All it was was an impossibility, something that somebody else does. It was a dream – I didn't believe it. I didn't know if I'd ever walk."

Terry could never explain why he set his sights on running across Canada, the second-largest country in the world. It didn't occur to him to dream of running in the New York Marathon or across British Columbia.

"I don't know why I dreamed what I did," he said. "It's because I'm competitive. I like challenges. I don't give up. That's why. When I decided to do it, I knew I was going to go all out. There was no in-between."

His parents and brother Fred were at the hospital at 6:00 a.m. on March 9 when Judith Ray arrived. Terry's surgery, scheduled for 8:00 a.m., would be the first of the day. Terry immediately showed Ray the magazine Terri Fleming had given him the night before. "Someday I'm going to do something like that," he said.

Terry had been thoroughly examined to see if there were any other tumours. Doctors checked his lungs especially carefully: if the sarcoma cells were going to spread, the lungs were the most likely site. Confident the cancer was contained, the doctors proceeded to amputate Terry's leg above the knee instead of at the hip, which would have been a more crippling procedure.

Despite his doctors' caution, it's likely stray sarcoma cells, carried in his bloodstream, were already resting in his lungs. As Louis Lichtenstein noted in his medical textbook *Bone Tumors*: "The discouraging outlook in dealing with osteogenic sarcoma does not appear to be attributable to any significant delay in its clinical recognition. What seems more probable, unfortunately, is that many patients with osteogenic sarcoma already have pulmonary seeding by the time they present themselves for treatment, even though their chest films appear negative."

The operation lasted about an hour. Terry's family doctor, Robert Heffelfinger, assisted Piper.

Terry didn't see what remained of his leg for a few days because it was wrapped in bandages. When the bandages were removed he saw a stump, "swollen, awful, in sad shape." A tube to drain fluid had been inserted from his groin down to the suture that enclosed the muscle and skin around the end of the bone.

Dr. Piper came several days later to check the amputation. Without a word of warning he ripped the tube out of Terry's leg. "I think that second of pain was the most excruciating pain I've ever been in and I just went 'whew' and he just patted me on the back."

His parents, perhaps, didn't accept the tragedy as readily as did Terry, but they did their best to follow Terry's lead. They saved their tears for home. Betty might become a little teary once in a while when she went back to work at the card shop, but she wasn't the sort to break down in public.

It was difficult for her to talk about Terry, especially when a friend asked how he was doing, and she made an effort to be strong and not to show her upset to others.

Terry wore his first artificial limb less than three weeks after the amputation. It was a temporary prosthesis because his stump was changing shape. He wouldn't get a permanent limb, which cost about two thousand dollars, until the swelling stopped and the stump reached the size it was likely to remain. In the meantime, Terry learned to walk on the primitive prosthesis, which included a plastic bucket shaped to resemble his mid-thigh and a knee that was flexible, but lacked the springs his permanent leg would have. The stump was held in the socket by suction only: air pressure would build up and be released manually through a valve in the bucket. The children on his ward – one of them a boy who was in traction and couldn't walk for six weeks – watched as Terry learned to walk on his new leg.

"When I took the first step I felt as though I was stepping on air. It felt as if I was stepping on nothing, straight down. The first thing I said to myself was, 'How am I ever possibly going to walk?'" Then he went to the washroom, so the children on the ward couldn't watch him, and tried again, with crutches.

"I kept trying and trying until I could do more, I could feel more, I could step into it more, follow through more, until I could lift. Gradually I got to the point where I could use only one crutch and then only one cane. All the time we were waiting for the stump to shrink until I got my final leg."

Everyone kept looking for signs, for some understanding of how Terry was adjusting to his new condition. True to his nature, he didn't blame anyone, he didn't have nightmares, he didn't expect special privileges, he didn't withdraw and reject his old friends. He carried on. Doug, who had been expecting some signs of depression, found none: "His attitude seemed to be, it is gone, now get on with it."

Terri Fleming also noticed Terry's positive outlook, which likely contributed to his very rapid recovery. Terry was told his rehabilitation was one of the quickest they'd seen at the hospital.

"He took it so damn well," Fleming recalled. "I thought I'd see someone terrified, someone who had given up, but he just accepted it. He took it. I thought he was hiding it, that he was going to crack up, but he didn't."

Terry loved his time in the hospital: he got along well with Judith Ray, he enjoyed the children on the ward, he even liked the food. He'd do his homework, then go for physiotherapy and build up his strength.

"And then I got out of hospital. You know, I didn't want to leave the hospital. That's how much I loved it."

Three weeks after he started using his artificial limb Terry played pitch-and-putt golf with Rolly. The next challenge was an eighteen-hole golf course. Not long after that he would play twenty-seven holes in a day.

There were proud moments for his dad and Doug and for anyone who played golf with Terry in those early months. He was slow on the course, but he was getting very good at the game. It seemed to Doug that Terry could actually drive the ball farther than he could when he had had both legs, although, according to Doug, anyone who saw Terry would swear he was aiming for the trees when he was teeing off. "He looked funny, he looked as if he was lined up wrong," Doug remembered. "All the weight was on his left leg and he held his body at an angle. You'd think he was going to hit the ball the wrong way."

The usual post-surgery follow-up after the type of surgery Terry had is chemotherapy, which is intended to destroy any stray malignant cells before they multiply. Although doctors hadn't found any signs that the tumours had spread, without follow-up treatment, there would have been a 70-per-cent chance of recurrence. (The Mayo Clinic, which does not follow up with chemotherapy, reports a high, 50-per-cent cure rate after surgery only. Following treatment of Edward Kennedy, Jr., chemotherapy was popularized in the mid-1970s and now is the usual course of treatment in most hospitals.)

A couple of weeks after his operation, Terry was admitted to the British Columbia Cancer Control Agency, commonly called the cancer clinic, in Vancouver. He'd go every three weeks for about sixteen months for chemotherapy treatment.

He was put on an experimental program to determine the most effective way to administer two proven cancer-killing drugs, adriamycin and methotrexate. (Adriamycin is one of the anthra-cycline family of chemicals, while methotrexate is a folic-acid antagonist, which blocks the action of folic acid, a vitamin-like substance needed for cell growth.) The two could be alternated or a treatment of adriamycin could be followed by a treatment of methotrexate. Terry was given the alternating program.

Terry's hair fell out when he started chemotherapy. He always said he hated losing his hair more than he hated losing a leg. He bought an inexpensive wig to hide his baldness. The other side effect was nausea. Sometimes it lasted only overnight, but sometimes, with adriamycin in particular, it lasted several days. Some patients say it's like having the flu. His appetite would be dulled for three or four more days, and then he would have some time at home to build up strength.

His doctors also had to watch that the drugs weren't harming his disease-fighting white blood cells and platelet-forming cells. They had to maintain a delicate balance to keep the dosage strong enough to kill the cancerous cells but not the patient. The final, most frightening side effect, attributed to adriamycin, was increased risk of heart failure.

Terry went to the clinic the night before his methotrexate treatment – adriamycin was usually administered as a shot – and would be fed fluids intravenously to get his kidneys working. Methotrexate, administered intravenously, is highly toxic, and would be excreted through his kidneys and his urine. He also chewed sodium bicarbonate pills to make his urine more alkaline and reduce the chances of methotrexate crystals forming in his kidneys.

One gram would be enough to kill him, and he was given between ten and fifteen grams in each treatment – but the drug was followed several hours later by an antidote, called leukovorin rescue, which was also fed into his bloodstream.

"The first time I took methotrexate I wasn't sick. I just felt a little light-headed," Terry said. "After a while I got sicker and sicker. Even the sodium bicarbonate made me sick, and the leukovorin, when they started it two hours later, was getting me down."

Although Terry looked forward to his parents' visits, he didn't like them to come the first night of his treatment because he was too sick. After a while he would ask for an anti-nausea shot, which put him to sleep and took care of the first day. The second day, his parents would come and treat him to dinner at the Knight and Day, a restaurant on busy West Broadway.

The cancer clinic, where the presence of mortally ill patients was a grim reminder that two-thirds of cancer victims died of the disease, was a different world from the pediatric ward at the Royal Columbian. Judith Ray had warned Terry that it would be. Terry saw himself as the healthiest person in the clinic, but rather than crushing his spirit, the sight of others' suffering made him stronger and more compassionate. He took the treatment in a four-patient room divided only by curtains. While he drew the curtains for privacy when he was vomiting after chemotherapy treatment, some of the other patients didn't. Although the atmosphere was intended to be supportive, on the theory that it was better for the patient to be in a room where others were struggling with the same problems, Terry detested the openness. "You could hear their stories, you could hear what was happening to them, what their situation was, what their reactions with their families were, and I didn't like that. There was no privacy. When I got sick, I wanted to be sick by myself and I couldn't.

"You could hear doctors telling these guys, 'You've got a 15-per-cent chance to live,' and this type of thing. I really didn't like that part of the hospital for that reason. I spent as much time out of the room as I could.

"It was just a really dull, dull place, but I have nothing but respect for the doctors and nurses. They have a lot of courage, and there aren't a lot of miracles there."

Judith Ray told Terry to be ready for the side effects, but nothing could prepare him for what he called the "grossities" of

Terry, Darrell, and Fred Fox, Christmas 1964.

Terry on the weekend of the "Prince George to Boston Marathon." Rick Hansen is in the wheelchair.

Canapress

The Port Coquitlam Senior Secondary School basketball team. Terry is wearing number 4, holding the ball. His brother Fred is standing, middle row, far left; coach Terri Fleming is also in the middle row, far right.

From left to right: Terry, Darrell, Mitch Fiddick (a family friend), and Doug Alward, September 1979.

Terry with St. John's Mayor Dorothy Wyatt on April 12, 1980, the beginning of the Marathon of Hope.

Terry was given a police escort when he arrived in Ontario. Until then, he was extremely vulnerable on the highways. At times, drivers had tried to force him off the road.

While in Ottawa, Terry had to decide whether to use his leg or his prosthesis to kick off a Canadian Football League game. Ottawa Roughrider Gerry Organ looks on.

In July 1980, Terry showed Prime Minister Pierre Trudeau how his prosthesis worked in the Parliament buildings, Ottawa.

Thousands crowded into Nathan Phillips Square, Toronto, to see Terry.

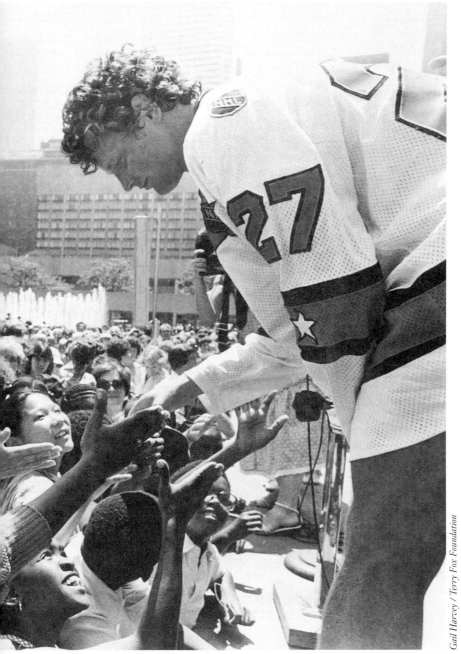

Hockey star Darryl Sittler gave him his 1980 All-Star team sweater.

Terry and Hockey legend
Bobby Orr compare knees.
Orr presented Terry
with a $25,000 check for
cancer research.

Terry was furious when a
newspaper reporter wrote a
story about the blood
leaking from his prosthesis.
"If I ran to a doctor every
time I got a little cyst or
abrasion, I'd still be
in Nova Scotia," he said.

Terry dries off after a swim in Jackfish Lake near Terrace Bay in Northern Ontario.

Terry swam with 10-year-old Greg Scott, who was undergoing chemotherapy for bone cancer.

Terry put in more miles in the early morning than at any other time
of day.

cancer: the swelling of a tumour on a young man's neck, the emaciation. "It shook him up," she said. "There were people in the same ward as him who had the same problem as he did, and it was obvious some of them were dying. That reinforced the reality of what he was up against. Even that didn't depress him. It gave him motivation to really fight, because he saw people there were really suffering. I suppose in a way it's unusual – he's a real natural fighter and worked hard for everything he's gotten or done – but there are a lot of people like that who, if you encourage them when they're down, are able to maintain that thrust forward."

During the weeks at home between treatments, Terry liked to keep life as normal as possible. Judith remembered playing ball with Terry in the backyard. "Since our family was really competitive, we threw the ball as hard as we could. When Terry missed a catch, the ball rolled under the trees and I ran to get it. He almost chewed my head off because it bothered him to think I had to help him. We didn't play ball for a while after that."

Betty bustled around the house trying to move things out of his way and cater to him as she never had before, spoiling him a little. She'd bring him food and drinks on a tray, though he was capable of getting them himself. He soon convinced her that he didn't need or want special treatment. He was so convincing that Darrell can hardly remember Terry being sick. He certainly never considered the possibility that his brother might not live.

Neither did his parents, even though they knew the odds against – about 50 per cent or greater – his survival. Whenever he went to a doctor's appointment, Betty and Rolly joined him. When he went to the cancer clinic, they went, too, asking questions all the time.

Although Terry may have seemed much the same to his younger brother, Terry experienced a profound change. He told a story about a twenty-two-year-old from the Okanagan who, for a while, shared his room at the clinic. He had Hodgkin's disease, a malignancy in the lymph glands, and he was riddled with tumours. "They gave him a chemotherapy treatment over the night, and the drug they gave him cleared his chest completely. It was just fantastic. He was so happy; they were letting him go home for a week. Then I saw the same guy about six months later . . . and he was just nothing. I was lying in my bed one night and I could hear a guy screaming in pain at different times. I got up to go to the washroom, and they were bringing him back in a wheelchair. He had tubes hooked up everywhere. I thought it was him and then I knew it was when I saw his name on an X-ray form. He was so thin and weak and fragile. He couldn't recognize me. He was probably drugged up. He was in a chair breathing, 'Help me, help me,' and that just hurt me. I saw that end of it a lot, but I hadn't seen the beginning. I hadn't seen the person healthy.

"There were a few other cases, too, people I'd seen progress. They were awful, sometimes, the stories. We talked about it. We had to talk, and it was hard, it was so hard – the pain in the faces and the situations people were in, with their families there and the whole thing.

"It's awful, but that's happening right now, all over the world in every city, in every town. That experience was really a motivator."

On the last day of his treatment, the nurses brought Terry a little cake and celebrated his release. Until that time, Terry's universe had been small. He had his basketball, his university work, good friends, and a close, caring family. He liked to watch the B.C. Lions and the Vancouver Canucks. He loved sports. He liked to go to the movies. He believed that most things in life – a good job, marriage, children – were within his grasp.

Terry often said he only thought of himself, but he was probably no more self-centred than any other teenager. He hadn't spent much time reflecting on the human condition. He had no reason for such thoughts. He was a nice, ordinary sort of teenager, honest, hardworking, disciplined, and well-mannered, but not unusually compassionate or caring. "I've always had a bad temper and I think I've hurt people at times because of it. When I was younger, especially before I had my cancer, maybe I'd take advantage of people. Even though I was motivated and I tried hard and did my best, made the SFU team and did well in school, I only did it because I wanted to achieve it myself. I would do anything, even hurt other people if I had to, to achieve that. But the clinic – that's what changed me."

Other cancer patients would show the same strength as Terry because their ordeal demanded that they be strong, but he took all his suffering, all that he had seen and heard, much further. He'd seen despair and not given in to it; he'd seen disease eat away at a young man's will to live, yet he felt mentally tougher than he had before cancer; and he'd faced death, yet was still alive. Believing he was among the lucky ones who survived cancer, Terry was transformed. He left the clinic with much more than a piece of cake and a round of thank-yous to the doctors and nurses who had treated him.

He felt a new sense of responsibility. He was among the one-third who survived cancer and he knew he had to lead his life in a different way. He believed in the value of cancer research. After all, thanks to advances in research and the new treatment he'd received, he was alive. He learned that cancer research was poorly funded in Canada and at university wrote papers on the subject. Since he had his life and had regained his health, he believed he had a debt to pay, not just for himself, but for all the others who came behind him and took his place in cancer wards. Terry became more than compassionate, he became inspired, and from that moment on vowed that others would find courage in the way he lived his life.

"Nobody," he said, "is ever going to call me a quitter."

5

"I JUST WANTED TO COMPETE
AGAINST SOMEONE"

Rick Hansen was uneasy about making the call. He'd heard about the Simon Fraser University basketball player who had lost a leg, and wondered if Terry would be interested in playing wheelchair basketball for the Vancouver Cablecars. That summer of 1977, Rick was working for the Canadian Wheelchair Sports Association, and part of his job was to recruit players. Sometimes it wasn't easy. He could never tell how a recent amputee would react to the idea of wheelchair sport.

Hansen saw the sport as a tough discipline, as challenging as any played by able-bodied athletes. Hansen, a paraplegic who could walk with crutches, but mainly used a wheelchair, was a superb athlete. He was similar to Terry in many ways. He was smart, hardworking, and set high standards for himself. He pushed himself twenty miles a day in his wheelchair. In later years, he won nineteen international wheelchair marathons, competed for Canada in the 1984 Los Angeles Olympics, and in 1985 began a two-year journey to wheel the circumference of the earth. Hansen wheeled forty thousand kilometres and

generated $36 million for spinal-cord research, for which he
became Canada's leading spokesperson. He also founded the
Rick Hansen Institute at the University of British Columbia, a
research-funding organization.

From their first conversation, something clicked between
Hansen and Terry. Terry listened as Hansen explained that he
had been an athlete before his accident, and that now, though
he no longer used his legs, he was still an athlete. He suggested
Terry might want a little exercise and offered to bring a wheelchair for him to the next practice.

Terry was interested. He didn't use a wheelchair for mobil-
ity. His artificial limb served him perfectly. But he sensed in Rick
a quality that was so much a part of his own nature: Rick, too,
pushed himself to the limit.

When Terry went to the Renfrew Community Centre for
the next wheelchair-basketball practice, he arrived with Rolly,
Betty, and Judith. His family was behind him in more than spirit.
Peter Colistro, whose right leg was in a brace after polio and
who would later become Terry's close friend, was shocked at the
appearance of the newest team member. To Peter, Terry was so
white and thin he looked like a scarecrow. He seemed fourteen
or fifteen years old instead of nineteen. His hair was long,
stringy, and flat, the kind you'd see sticking out of a strawman's
hat. This was before he started chemotherapy.

Terry started practising lay-ups. He was a little shaky. He
was amazed, in fact, that the men could actually do basketball
drills from wheelchairs. On his first few tries, Terry couldn't
come close to the rim, but by the end of the practice he made
two lay-ups in a row. The other players saw immediately that
Terry had good skills. He just had to learn to alter his basketball
reflexes, which were directed to his legs, up to his arms. He was
always trying to jump to his feet to get the ball. Rick explained
that Terry had to redevelop his neuro-muscular pathways:

instead of moving with his feet, as his instinct told him, he had to move with his hands.

According to the modified rules for wheelchair basketball, he was allowed five seconds in the key instead of the usual three seconds, and he had to dribble the ball if he took more than two pushes on his wheelchair. He had to strap himself into the chair to keep from jumping for the ball. It reminded Terry of those days that seemed a lifetime away, when he was a grade-eight boy in Bob McGill's basketball practice. He had to learn a new skill and, this time, he was thirteenth man on a thirteen-man team. But nothing in Terry's character would let him be the weakest player for long. His soft palms toughened up. They blistered, and the blisters broke, bled, and then callused over.

Mike McNeill at SFU watched him as he worked to improve his skills in the wheelchair. Once McNeill caught Terry as he came into the gym and he stopped dead. "Jesus, Terry, look at your hands," he said. Terry looked down and saw the scrapes. Cuts ran across his palms, and his fingertips "were all chewed up." McNeill's concern baffled Terry. He was happy and it never occurred to him to complain – he was doing what he wanted.

Within two months of joining the Cablecars, Terry was picked to go to the national wheelchair-basketball games in Edmonton that August.

In those months he had climbed from thirteenth to sixth place on the team. Unbelievably, Terry was still taking chemotherapy. While he was in Edmonton, arrangements were made for Terry to take a chemotherapy treatment at the University of Alberta hospital. It was only when he went with Terry and talked to one of the doctors, that Peter Colistro learned about Terry's condition.

"Is he that bad, doc?" Colistro asked. The doctor replied that Terry was very sick and should never have travelled with the team to Edmonton. For the first time Colistro faced the shocking possibility that Terry might not have long to live. Everything fell into place: Terry's skeletal appearance, how he sometimes dozed off on the sidelines during a game, the doctor's concern.

Despite that, the Cablecars won the nationals – they claimed the title ten times in twelve years – and Terry helped them win. He eventually played on two more championship-winning teams.

Terry's teammates kept their worry about him to themselves. For his part, he never wanted sympathy and dreaded being treated differently. However, there was a slight problem with the wig. No one but Darrell, who once saw Terry in the shower, had ever seen him without it.

"I used to pat Terry on the head if he'd made a good play," said Rick Hansen, "and I thought it was strange that every time I patted him, he'd reach up and touch his hair. We went down to Portland for a tournament and were brutally beaten by Los Angeles in a preseason game. While we were showering I noticed that even though Terry was standing right under the water, his hair wasn't getting wet. Terry noticed me looking and said, 'I'm going to have to tell you something. You know when you pat me on the head? I don't want you to tell anyone, but I'm wearing a wig and I'm afraid you're going to knock it off!'

"From then on, I patted him on the shoulder. But about a month or so later, back home during a team practice, Terry was in the middle of a scramble for the ball and there were five guys around him. He had the ball and was moving around so no one could check him. One of the big guys, Gene Reimer, a weightlifter, took a swipe at the ball, and then all I saw was this wig come sailing out of the scrimmage. First came the wig, then came Terry, diving after it and plastering it on his head as fast as he could. His face was beet red." It was the most colour they'd seen in his face since he joined the team. There was a moment of uncomfortable silence. Do you ignore it? Do you laugh? They laughed, and Terry laughed loudest.

When his hair started growing back, first as a light fuzz, Terry wore a baseball cap, and had trouble with one referee who objected to a player wearing a hat. Terry was so upset, he didn't play well.

Soon Terry began motivating the other wheelchair-basketball players. His competitive spirit spurred the same instincts in Hansen, Colistro, and their teammates. He pestered them, he pushed them, he irritated them. He called them slackers, and his intensity inspired everyone. Because he was a student at SFU, he arranged gym time so the wheelchair players could practise more. He couldn't understand that some of the men on the team were in the game just for fun.

His body changed, too. His hair grew back, this time in luxuriant curls. His torso thickened and became muscular. He had changed, Rick recalled, "from a skinny little runt to a strapping fellow with lots of beef and muscle." He also had his own wheelchair for basketball, a gift from Rolly's work mates in the Canadian National Railway yard.

By the 1979-80 season, the Cablecars were rated sixth in the North American Wheelchair Basketball Association. Both Terry and Colistro were chosen as guards for the all-star team. It was an honour, but Terry, as usual, felt he could have played better.

Later, at the 1980 Wheelchair Olympics, held in Arnhem, Holland, Colistro was chosen for the all-star team. He was ranked one of the five best wheelchair players in the world. He gave credit to Terry, among others, for helping him achieve that standard of excellence. In the same competition Hansen set a world record in the eight-hundred-metre sprint in his wheelchair and won a gold medal.

Terry played wheelchair basketball three nights a week, but he was used to a more challenging régime so he devised one himself. By mid-1978 he was pushing himself hard to strengthen his arms and hands. He'd go anywhere that offered a challenge.

Some days found him hurtling along the sea wall around Vancouver's Stanley Park. He set out past the marina near the lavish Bayshore Hotel and circled round until he could see Burrard Inlet, which stretched long and far down to Port Moody. He pushed past the statue of the Little Mermaid, and then continued under the great arch of the Lions Gate Bridge. To his left loomed centuries-old stands of fir and cedar, and to his right were the great freighters, the fishing boats, and tugs chugging towards the Vancouver docks. It was perhaps one of the loveliest walks in Canada, a favourite of joggers, cyclists, and visitors from around the world. To Terry, those joggers and strollers were markers and challenges; he had to wheel by them as fast as he could.

Even that wasn't enough for Terry. He went looking for a mountain to conquer and found Westwood Mountain. It was a steep hill near his house, rarely used and more challenging than the sea wall. A road led to a go-cart and automobile track; the top had been logged, and the heavy trucks had cut up the surface, making driving rough and slow.

Sometimes Rolly would drop Terry at the bottom of the hill and wait in the car for him at the top. Terry might wheel himself up the hill two or three times in one session. His best time was fifteen minutes.

Once in a while, Doug Alward, who was training for cross-country running, would run with him to the top. It wasn't exactly a race, but it gave Terry someone to measure himself against. "I just wanted to compete against someone," Terry said. "I didn't want to compete just against the hill. Knowing that Doug – or anyone, even a dog – was coming up behind me was just what I needed to go my hardest. I used him to push me harder."

Nonetheless, it must have been a startling scene: Terry breathing hard and heavy after a head start, his strong arms pushing the wheels, and Doug setting out a few minutes later, doing his damnedest to conquer that mile and possibly Terry.

From the top, on clear days, Terry could see the snowcapped cone of Mount Baker in Washington State on the horizon. Sometimes the whole valley, a blanket of evergreen, stretched out before him; other times the lowlands were hidden in fog. Mostly, though, it just rained, and Terry, drenched and determined, kept on wheeling.

His third challenge was Burnaby Mountain. For nearly three miles, a road winds up the mountain to Simon Fraser University. It's named Gaglardi Way, after a former minister of transport in the B.C. government, and cuts a four-lane swath through the spindly birch that in mild winters will stay green until December. It's not as steep as Westwood Mountain, but it's three times as long, and the broken-down Volkswagens abandoned by the side of the road show that not all who attempt the mountain make it to the top.

Students driving to the library or gym on weekends would have noticed peculiar movement on the side of the road. One described it as a moving box, until he got close enough to recognize Terry in his wheelchair. Terry's best time was about thirty minutes, which he could check against the clock tower when he reached the top of the hill. Sometimes he'd ask one of his friends to drive him back to his car at the bottom of the hill because his hands would be rubbed raw trying to hold back the wheelchair on a downward slope. "Sometimes I was stupid and I'd do it on my own," said Terry. "Sometimes I'd come down in the pouring rain and couldn't get a grip on the wheels. They just slipped through my hands. Once I hitchhiked down. I just sat in the wheelchair and stuck out my thumb. The first guy who passed me stopped."

Terry didn't understand why this part of his story made such a impression on anyone who heard it. He was an athlete and this is what athletes did. It was nothing special. He saw that long, daunting climb as just another part of his training. It was no more of an achievement than the dull hours he spent circling the

SFU gym in his wheelchair. All he remembered was that he was training alone, without a coach, without one of his motivators, going around and around and around the empty gym with a single-minded dedication that had become his trademark.

Terry tried running next. He remembered his first attempt at competitive running: "I was going to run a hundred metres, and a guy named Dan, who's a double amputee and uses crutches, was going to crutch a hundred metres. But since there were two of us they threw us in the same heat. Even though we were in different competitions, we were put in the same heat.

"I ran as fast as I could go – and I can run fast, can get going pretty good when I just sprint, you know – and my knee broke right in half, and I went flying after only about ten metres and I landed on the ground. Danny went by me, crutching away. It took him about a minute and a half to finish a hundred metres and he said, 'At least I beat Terry.' That was funny."

About this time Terry met Rika Noda, a Japanese-Canadian stained-glass artist. Rika had a little studio built in the back of her bedroom in the basement of her parents' split-level house overlooking the Fraser River. Her stained-glass works were whimsical; one of them illustrated the Hickory Dickory Dock nursery rhyme, with mice, and red hearts dangling from the chimes of the grandfather clock. She still kept stuffed toys, including a Snoopy, tossed on her bed, not far from the bookshelf filled with Bibles, books on spirituality and sports. She was taking a course in recreational leadership at Langara College. Like Terry, she seemed younger than her twenty years. She was petite and vivacious and her liveliness contrasted with Terry's shyness.

Rika heard about Terry some time before she met him. She was an assistant coach for the Canadian Wheelchair Volleyball Association. Some of the volleyball players also played basketball and told her about the SFU basketball player who was now playing well for the wheelchair team. One evening the volleyball players took Rika to the Renfrew Community Centre to watch a basketball game. She spotted Terry immediately. He was the one, in her eyes, who seemed to be playing harder and better than the others. She didn't fail to notice, either, that he was good-looking.

He noticed her, too, and within a few weeks started playing wheelchair volleyball, though his interest in volleyball waned while his interest in Rika grew. He would drive her home from practice, and one night shyly and formally asked her to dinner at the Sears Harbour House.

Rika, a girl who felt most comfortable in jeans or corduroy overalls and sneakers, and who was happiest doing her work sitting cross-legged on the floor, was surprised at how solemn Terry was when he invited her, but quickly accepted. She had found a dress to wear for the night, and as they walked to the elevator of the revolving restaurant, Terry took her hand. The city of Vancouver was at their feet. They continued to hold hands and spoke not of how they felt about one another, but of a topic close to Rika's heart – God's love.

Rika was a Christian. Terry had ridiculed the "television Christians" whose ministries are conducted, as he said, with "perfect hairdos, perfect clothes, and perfect plastic smiles." He didn't like the praise-the-Lord approach to divinity, but he was interested in Rika's style of Christianity. She believed in God, that Christ had died for all mankind, and that the Bible held the key to eternal life. She was warm, exuberant, and wasn't aggressively trying to convert him.

Just as Terry had been sent to Sunday School as a child, Rika had been sent to a Buddhist temple. Later, she attended Christian services. She said she became a Christian when she was nine and had a child's faith but lacked adult understanding.

That came later, when she experienced a "sanctification," as she called it, and developed a "personal relationship with God." As she grew closer to Terry, she hoped that he would experience the same illumination, not only for his own sake but also because she believed that, as a Christian, she should not go out with boys who had not embraced Christ as she had. But she was drawn to Terry, with his competitive instincts and shy manner. She found him irresistible.

Terry was also drawn to Rika and what she had to say. She started taking him to the Ruth Morton Baptist Church, which she attended. Sunday was the busiest day of her week. Rika urged Terry to read the Bible and he did. She was one of the few people to whom he could talk about cancer. Cancer and his experiences at the clinic had introduced a new, thoughtful side to Terry. Though he was still young, he was probing for answers to life's deepest questions.

"I guess I was searching for something, for an answer," he said. "I had just finished treatment and had a lot of questions: Why did I get cancer and not someone else? I was starting to think about life. I was getting older, too, thinking about different attitudes towards life. I didn't know how I could apply those attitudes in my life. I was looking for an answer to the question why."

While Rika was directing Terry on his spiritual path, he felt torn, divided between his old loyalties and his new ones. None of his friends was an active believer. His parents were not churchgoers.

"I worried about what my family thought. Even if I wanted to change my life, none of my friends was interested in it, and I couldn't forget about them all. I couldn't block them out. I wanted them. Yet I almost felt I had to do that – block them out – to devote myself to it. It's always difficult to be different from the norm. To me, just starting to read the Bible was different from what anyone else in my family was doing."

Throughout these months, Terry harboured his dream of running across Canada, but, as he said, it wasn't the right time. He was strong, but he had run very little and had yet to develop his stamina. The most rigorous training of his life lay before him.

6

"MOM, I'M GOING TO RUN

ACROSS CANADA"

In January 1979, Terry started a diary. It was a plain, pocket-sized notebook covered in vinyl. He wrote his name, address, SFU student number, and phone number on the front cover. Terry didn't reflect about life or himself in its pages. He always insisted he didn't write well, though his writing often showed clarity and flashes of insight. His first entries were a daily reminder and record of his school assignments:

January 4. Scholarship. Books. Basketball. Phone auto places.

January 14. Continue Kin. 467 reading. Basketball. Think about 320 essay if can't figure out, see T.A. on Tuesday.

January 27. Kin. 467 reread chapter, underline reread notes, memorize, continue lab.

February 10. Wheel up mountain. Bring Rika get her to type essay.

Gradually, Terry began to record his running. He didn't write down his first quarter-mile effort, in the rain, around a muddy track, but the entry from February 15 read: "1/2 mile, weights."

Terry ran his first half-mile around the cinder track at Hastings Junior High School, where Judith went to school. It was about six blocks from his home. Four laps around the track, which was lined on three sides with tall stands of fir, equalled one mile. "It was hard, it was hard. The first few half-miles especially. I remember on my third time or so, I was just dead, completely dead. Sweating, wiped out. I would usually run at night then."

Seven days later Terry ran his first mile. "The first day I ran a mile was as great as the first day I ran thirty miles because to me it was phenomenal. Here I was, getting healthy and active and getting strong and running hard. In shorter distances you naturally run faster. In fact, one day I remember running past two-legged people who were jogging. That helped me and made me feel great. You know, I enjoyed it. I really was glad I was able to do that.

"I was weightlifting as well, at the time, and I was building my strength up. My body was getting bigger, my leg was getting bigger. I was getting healthier and in better condition and feeling more positive all the time. Each time I ran a further distance, when I was able to run a further half-mile, it was great because I was improving all the time and I was able to keep going."

Terry worked with his prosthetist Ben Speicher on developing a better running leg. Speicher devised a pogo stick with a motorcycle's shock absorber to give Terry more oomph with each step, but Terry didn't like it, so they reverted to a more traditional leg reinforced and modified to endure long-distance running. The metal valve in the bucket was replaced with one of stainless steel so it wouldn't rust from perspiration. Speicher added a belt that fitted around Terry's waist and attached to an elastic strap at the knee to bring the leg forward more quickly after each stride. Despite that adjustment, Terry had to take two steps with his good leg in the time it took the artificial leg to swing around.

In addition to the ordinary fatigue felt by two-legged runners, Terry had special problems. His good leg suffered from the extra pounding he gave it. He developed blisters on his foot and cysts on his stump.

"I had some bad blisters, man. Oh boy, it was just like running on hot coals. I really had some sores on my leg where the artificial leg was. They just rubbed raw and there's no protection at all. Sometimes the sores would bleed right through the valve in the bucket and the blood would run all down my knee and my leg and I had it all over me."

Sometimes adjusting his leg to a more comfortable position would bring some relief, but he was always searching for just the right technique, the right motion that would make running easier and the pain less intense.

"One of the harder times was when I went from running on cinder track to cement, because running on cement was so hard on my body, especially my foot. I developed bone bruises. My toe and heel were totally blistered, like raw, and I lost three toenails all because of running on cement. I had shin splints for two months, a sharp pain in my lower leg. I did it all gradually. If I hadn't I would have probably broken my leg. I was fortunate. Here was where stubbornness came through. I knew the toenails would grow back in and would be okay. The blisters, I knew, were eventually going to turn to calluses, but I was afraid of the bone bruise because I could have gotten stress fractures. But I kept going and it went away.

"Usually the pain came in different stages. A lot of times the very beginning is the hard part. You have to take the first fifteen or twenty minutes to get warmed up. Then you get over a pain threshold. That's what I did a lot. You'd still have the pain and blisters, and sometimes it would get a little worse and then not so bad again, but it never was unbearable. There were times when it really hurt, but I kept going. I can't remember ever being in so much pain for such a long time that I had to stop. I never did."

Through these months, only Doug knew that Terry was dreaming of running across Canada. Doug, meanwhile, was training for the "Prince George to Boston Marathon," held on Labour Day weekend. It was neither a marathon nor a cross-continent run. The race was seventeen miles and the runner with the best time earned a ticket to the Boston Marathon. Terry had phoned Doug in the spring and asked for general advice about running and sometimes they would run together.

Doug recalled, "He wanted my advice, but wouldn't listen to it. I thought he ate too much meat and salad: you can't get calories from that. He was stubborn and we'd fight and argue, but after a while he might bend a bit. His dream of running across Canada didn't seem odd to me. He just told me what he wanted to do, and then we started talking about training.

"I guess I never looked at him as having an artificial leg. Having one leg may have made it a little more difficult, but when Terry said he was going to do something, he did it. After all, he made the basketball team. He wasn't one to make phony promises. If anyone could run across Canada, he could. But I didn't think training would be as difficult as it was. Even I didn't know what it was like to run twenty miles a day. At my best, when I was training for Prince George, I ran up to sixty miles a week."

Later, Terry told Rika he had an idea that he would run across Canada. Both his friends seemed to have accepted Terry's goal uncritically. Rika, used to Terry's enthusiasm and determination, also believed Terry could do it. "He had to do something so monumental to prove to himself more than anything else that he could do it. Of course, he wanted to raise money for cancer, but I think more than anything it was a really big personal battle."

Rika was troubled by their relationship. She loved Terry, but now understood he didn't feel the same way. He told her he didn't have the time to spend with a girlfriend because he had to concentrate on running. He still enjoyed her company and hoped they could be friends. Rika, however, felt he sometimes took advantage of her good nature, especially when he picked her up, took her to his house, and set her to work typing his English essays while he watched television. Terry was shocked and hurt by the notion that Rika felt used. "I believed she wanted to help me because she was my friend," he said.

Rika, like Betty Fox, found it difficult to get angry with Terry. She liked his honesty and spontaneous, though some-times explosive, emotions. Beneath his grumpiness she saw a certain purity and she didn't want to lose him. She knew the relationship was unequal, but she continued to spend time with Terry because she was still so fond of him.

By June, Terry realized his priorities had shifted so much that, even with Rika's help, he was falling behind in his class-work. He was still a high achiever and he didn't want to drop too far behind. He gave himself a pep talk in his diary: "Get to work at 401 lab. Let's do it, Terry, it is important. As important as running." He followed that sentence with a row of big, fat exclamation points.

By August 11, Terry was running ten miles a day and had lost two toenails. He could race up Westwood Mountain twice in succession, and some days he would alternate that with a seven-mile evening run around Stanley Park.

On August 30, Terry left with Doug, Darrell, Rika, and a young friend, Mitch Fiddick, for the Prince George race. He planned to run the eight-and-a-half-mile race because so far he hadn't run more than eleven miles in one day, but Doug was picking away at him to run the seventeen-mile course.

Doug's soft voice got under his skin. He kept asking Terry why he only wanted to run eight and a half miles: he could run that at home any day he wanted. Why travel five hundred miles to do something that he could do at home? Why not make it an event? Why not try for seventeen miles? Terry went for it again.

Doug came eighth in the race, with one of his best times. Darrell placed second in the junior race. Terry came last, with a time of three hours, nine minutes, running at the impressive rate of eleven minutes for each mile. What made him beam with pride was that the last two-legged runner was only ten minutes ahead of him. Some of the organizers worried about Terry's running so many miles and debated whether they should force him to stop. They didn't ask him to stop, and Terry insisted that, even if they had, nothing could have held him back. Nothing.

No one could have deprived him of that moment when he crossed the finish line and a crowd of maybe a hundred people stood to cheer and honour him. Terry's confidence was unshakeable after that. He never doubted his abilities, but when he heard their shouts of praise, when he saw fellow athletes weeping, he saw for the first time that each of his steps carried an emotional punch. That night at the awards banquet, the winner said what affected him most was the sight of the tough little amputee runner.

When they arrived home from Prince George, Betty walked out to the driveway to welcome them. Terry was still jubilant. That reunion in the driveway showed how close Betty and Terry were. Long afterward, telling the story to others, Betty's eyes would fill with tears and the words would catch in her throat. She remembered Terry's excitement and how he couldn't tell her quickly enough all that had happened.

Then he said to her, "I wish you'd been there, Mom. It was the biggest day of my life!" Betty wondered, for a long time after, why she and Rolly hadn't gone to watch him.

A few days later, back home, Terry and Doug were driving along the Barnet Highway into Vancouver to go to the movies. Terry said that he thought he was ready to try the cross-Canada run. Doug, calm, practical, almost immovable, said, "When?" That's all. Originally they had thought it would take two years of training, but Terry was bursting with confidence and strength, and two years seemed an awfully long time. Then Doug suggested, simply, "Why not try for next spring?" It seemed so clear and they agreed. Terry took three days' rest and then started running again. This time he was training to run across Canada.

Those were difficult days. Terry had to break the news to Betty and Rolly, who still didn't know what he was planning. He went to his mother first. It was the end of the day. He had run ten miles that morning and had another four-and-a-half to run when he finished speaking to his mother. Betty remembers standing at the kitchen sink when Terry came in. He stood at the end of the counter and blurted out his story. "I was absolutely floored by what he said," Betty reported.

The conversation went something like this:

"Mom, I'm going to run across Canada."

"You are not."

"Yes, I am."

"Terry, you are not!"

Terry shouted that he was going to do it anyway and it would be better if she was behind him.

Betty remembered the next part. "I probably told him it was a dumb, crazy idea. Why not run across B.C.? Run marathons. He went out madder than a hatter, slamming the door behind him."

It was left up to Betty to tell Rolly. She waited a few days and then, in a quiet moment, went down to the family room.

"Sit there and listen," she said to Rolly. "Don't yell." Then she told him about Terry's plans.

Rolly, who had sensed that something important was being kept from him, only said, "When?" He knew Terry too well for this to be an idle dream. What else was there to say?

By now, Betty was convinced that she was the only one in the family with any common sense. She wondered if Terry really knew how much work and money it would take to run across Canada. Apparently he did. He had discussed his idea with Colin Johnstone, chaplain at the cancer clinic, and on the same day had walked into the office of Blair MacKenzie, executive director of the British Columbia and Yukon Division of the Canadian Cancer Society, and told him he wanted to raise money for cancer research. MacKenzie was sceptical. Every year, a few men and women would approach the society asking for sponsorship, but MacKenzie usually found there were strings attached. To test their sincerity, he told them the society would give them no financial support, but that if they found sponsors they would talk further. Usually MacKenzie never heard from them again.

MacKenzie believed Terry's ambition, to raise one million dollars, was impossible.

Terry left MacKenzie a letter, one that he composed with Rika – using his ideas and her grammar. His letter read:

The night before my amputation, my former basketball coach brought me a magazine with an article on an amputee who ran in the New York Marathon. It was then when I decided to meet this new challenge head on and not only overcome my disability, but conquer it in such a way that I could never look back and say it disabled me. But I soon realized that would only be half of my quest, for as I went through the sixteen months of the physically and emotionally draining ordeal of chemotherapy, I was rudely awakened by the feelings that surrounded and coursed throughout the cancer clinic. There were the faces with the brave smiles, and the ones who had given up smiling. There were the feelings of hopeful denial, and the feelings of despair. My quest would not be a selfish one. I could not leave knowing these faces and feelings would still exist, even though I would be set free from mine. Somewhere the hurting must stop . . . and I was determined to take myself to the limit for this cause. . . .

By April next year I will be ready to achieve something that for me was once only a distant dream reserved for the world of miracles; to run across Canada to raise money for the fight against cancer. . . . I'm not saying that this will initiate any kind of definitive answer or cure to cancer, but I believe in miracles. I have to.

MacKenzie also told Terry that he had to check with his Cancer Society superiors, a delay that frustrated Terry, who didn't want to go home and wait. Nonetheless, the task MacKenzie set him was simple. With his mother, Terry composed a second letter, which they sent to Imperial Oil, the Ford Motor Company, Adidas, and several other companies, asking for gas, a vehicle, running shoes, and money respectively.

He sent other letters to organizations asking for grants to buy a running leg: "Today I feel privileged to even be alive. But as I think back to those first few months how scared I was, not knowing whether I would live or die, I remember promising myself that, should I live, I would rise up to meet this new challenge face to face and prove myself worthy of life, something too many people take for granted."

He said he had to act immediately: "I cannot stand to see life pass by so quickly without some kind of accomplishment, some meaningful milestone to set down to show that someone can do it, or at least give it his best shot. Already much time has gone by and my sense of urgency grows stronger with each passing day."

Terry became more driven, more irritable, and more stubborn than anyone imagined possible. He'd pick Betty up after work, and as she sat beside him in the car she'd see blood oozing out of the valve and down his knee. His socks would be drenched in blood. She bit her lip to keep from crying or saying anything that might upset him. She knew from experience that the wrong word would set off Terry's temper like fireworks, so she said nothing.

Sometimes she felt Terry was nasty in his obsession to run, but she understood that he often acted without thinking. Besides, she thought, that temperament ran in the family. He was never malicious, or deliberately unkind, it was just that he wanted life to go smoothly. If it didn't he was irritated. In his family, where tempers exploded easily and where shouting matches were common, Terry's stubborn single-mindedness was tolerated, but grudgingly.

Rika, who spent much of her free time at Terry's house, often welcomed him home after his first run of the day. She, too, felt his anger. She said he purposely left his bloodied leg on for three or four hours before going out for the second run. His mother tried to warn him that he risked infection, but he didn't listen and refused to discuss his pain.

Perhaps no one can ever know the pressure Terry felt during those days. No one could understand how he had to toughen himself to run when every human instinct told him to stop and care for his injuries. Betty saw more of his suffering than anyone else in the family, but she couldn't help him with his burden. Soon, she found it impossible to watch Terry run.

One of Terry's secrets was that he set small goals for himself. He didn't think about running ten miles when he set out in the morning. Instead, he ran one mile at a time. "I broke it down. Get that mile down, get to that sign, get past that corner and around that bend. That's all it was. That's all I thought about. I didn't think of anything else."

Terry's route took him through Ioco, the company town built for employees of the Imperial Oil refinery. He ran past cozy middle-class houses with wood siding and car ports, past Burrard Inlet and the smoke of the refinery; he ran up hills to Sasamat Lake, which is the same deep blue-green as the mountains reflected in its water. The weather was always damp. Moss crawled over graffiti on the rocks, and the telephone wires always sparkled with raindrops.

To help him forget the pain in his stump and foot, Terry counted telephone poles and played mathematical games, calculating how far he'd come and how far he had yet to go. Whenever he saw people ahead of him, he sped up to pass them. If he was going to run, he was going to run with style and speed. "People helped me. People got to know me on the run. I'd say hi to them as I got to know them, especially the people in Ioco. I got to know mailmen and milkmen. I got to know all the truck drivers on that ten-mile route." He remembered the tiny elderly woman in the blue coat and fur collar he passed nearly every day. She walked slowly, but they always exchanged a cheery word. Sometimes, though, he had the greatest effect on those he never met. One woman who had watched him run wrote this letter:

In January 1979, we moved to Port Moody and I started a 6:30 a.m. routine driving our little dog to a deserted area along the newly constructed road, the extension of Ioco east, to let him have his run. This is when I first saw you "in training" and simply could not believe my eyes. Even though I am in good health and have two good legs, there I was driving the car. You shamed me into buying a warm-up suit and jogging shoes. Unfortunately, jogging to me is the most torturous form of exercise.

My routine didn't last too long. But there you were, morning after morning in sleet and snow and cold rain keeping up a continuous arduous pace – wearing shorts while I shivered driving along beside our dog.

During those first months, Terry, there was so much agony in your face, but so much determination, too. I wanted to stop and say how much [my son] Michael and I admired your effort. I was so overwhelmed it may have created embarrassment for you . . .

Through the summer I saw you several times, sweat pouring down your face. One very hot day, I wanted to stop to offer a ride, get a cool drink, anything to get you out of the heat. Once I circled the area three times just to make sure you were going to make it along that lone deserted stretch of road.

In late summer and fall we missed seeing you, but when you suddenly appeared again we could see the tremendous improvements. Your leg was almost twice the size, very muscular and strong. Your whole body looked stronger and you moved easier without showing stress and pain. Indeed you looked very happy, justifiably pleased with your progress.

(Signed) Shelagh and Michael.

On his ten- and fifteen-mile runs, Terry looked on that stretch of road as if it were his own. "It was my ten miles. I knew it better than anybody. I knew every niche and crack in the road. You couldn't find a better ten miles in the world."

There were days, of course, that he wanted to give up and nearly did. He suffered bouts of diarrhea and shivered with cold sweats. Along the sea wall at Stanley Park, he'd buck the wind. The next day would be bright and sunny, and his resilient body would rejoice with speed and energy. It was always changing. One day just before Christmas, when he had gone only a half-mile, the lower half of his artificial leg broke in two, sending him sprawling on the pavement. He gathered his dignity and his leg and, holding the parts in his hand, hitchhiked home. Then he clamped the leg together and ran another five miles.

Three days later he wrote in his diary: "Christmas Day, day of rest." He had run 101 days in a row and stopped only on Christmas Day at his mother's request.

In January, Terry missed his three-month appointment for a chest X-ray at the cancer clinic. "I just didn't think I needed it. I was really, really busy. Almost always if the cancer spreads it spreads in the first six or nine months. I really did not believe the cancer would come back."

Terry hated the X-rays. "Every time I went down, I was shivering and it wasn't because I was cold. I was afraid."

Certain that he had been cured, Terry directed every thought, every action to his running. He had asked Rika to join him on the run. Although still loyal to him, Rika was wary because she found herself going home in tears too many nights. It was clear something between them had changed. Confused, Rika asked for help from the pastor at her church. He advised her not to go on the run because, although she and Terry knew the limits of their relationship, not everyone would understand. Living in such close quarters with two men would lessen her credibility as a Christian, he told her.

A few months before they were scheduled to leave, Doug had second thoughts. He was shy and introverted and wondered if Terry shouldn't find someone better qualified to help, maybe

someone who would be more comfortable with reporters, or
better able to do fundraising on the road, or even someone who
could help Terry with his injuries or the stresses of running. He
asked himself, Did he really want to sit in a van for seven
months? Then he thought, if anyone could sit in a van for seven
months, "it was me." He tried to back down, but Terry insisted
and Doug's parents thought the trip would help him learn to be
comfortable with people.

"One thing about Doug," Terry said, "I knew I could depend
on him. When he gave his word, you knew he would stick by it.
I knew he was somebody who would not give up. We'd been
friends for a long, long time. He knew a lot about running tech-
niques and injuries. He knew a whole lot about the whole run.
He could stand a long situation without things changing and I
knew that. I thought we could get along well together for a long
time. I thought the trip would help him a lot."

Soon the plans started taking shape. Ford had agreed to
supply a camper van, which Doug would drive. Adidas came
through with running shoes for both Doug and Terry. Imperial
Oil offered five hundred dollars in gas money and Canada
Safeway donated the same amount in cash and food vouchers.
Pacific Western Airlines offered transportation to Winnipeg,
and private donors paid the rest of the airfare to St. John's.
Labatt's Brewery donated beer for a dance the Fox family organized at the Port Coquitlam Recreation Centre, which raised
$2,500 to help pay for living expenses along the way. War
Amputations of Canada offered to repair or replace Terry's pros-
thesis as necessary.

A tentative itinerary was made up, with St. John's as the
starting point. If Terry left there on April 12 and ran thirty miles
or more daily – a surprising target since he'd run no more than
twenty-three miles a day at home – he would arrive at Port
Renfrew on the west coast of Vancouver Island September 10.

The national office of the Canadian Cancer Society agreed to promote the run, although organizers were still sceptical of its success. Terry's run would follow the society's busy spring fundraising season, and they worried that the volunteers, who would be suffering from post-campaign fatigue, would not be willing to start up again and rally again behind the Cancer Society symbol.

Nearly everything was in place. All he needed now was a medical certificate from a heart specialist saying that he was in sufficiently good health to attempt the run. That request came from Dr. Robert Macbeth, executive vice-president of both the Cancer Society and the National Cancer Institute of Canada, the society's research arm.

That last hurdle was the most difficult. One week before Terry was to board a plane for St. John's, he saw Dr. Akbar Lalani, a New Westminster heart specialist. Terry had already decided that, no matter what the doctor said, he was going to run. But he also knew he had developed a condition known among athletes as an enlarged heart and among specialists as left ventricular hypertrophy. Terry's condition was slightly different from the condition commonly associated with athletes because only the left ventricle, not his whole heart, was enlarged.

Doctors are still not sure whether Terry's condition was related to use of the drug adriamycin during chemotherapy, whether it was merely an athletic condition, or whether it was the result of a congenital malformation. Terry thought the problem was linked to the drug treatment.

Lalani told Terry, "'Something could go wrong with you tomorrow, yet you're in the top physical shape. Right now you're doing all this activity, your heart's taking it, but you might die tomorrow because of it. But what will probably happen is that you'll live to be seventy years old.' It was abnormal but it wasn't really threatening at the time. He couldn't say whether something would happen or not. So I was sitting there. I didn't know whether the condition was going to affect me or not.

"He said to me, 'Why don't you run across B.C. first?' But I had already run more than three thousand miles proving myself. Why run across B.C. first?"

Lalani found Terry "agitated" and understandably very keen to start his run. He knew that Terry would run with or without his permission. He gave it reluctantly.

He warned Terry that if he felt he was experiencing any problems with his heart he should stop running immediately. Lalani cautioned him to beware of dizzy spells, shortness of breath, and rapid tiring. He suggested that Terry had set himself too great a task by hoping to run up to thirty miles a day. He said ten miles daily would be safer.

Terry must have paled when he heard the symptoms associated with heart failure. He had already experienced them, and he had told no one but Rika, whom he had sworn to secrecy. Terry had thought the dizziness and double vision he had felt while running were connected with the heat.

Rika worried that Terry was too sick to begin the run. "Once he told me he was seeing ten images at once. It was difficult not to say anything. Was I being irresponsible by ignoring a bigger problem or was I being a faithful friend?" She was powerless against Terry's single-minded sense of purpose. "Stubborn doesn't describe it. That word seems so small next to him."

Just before he left for St. John's he felt those symptoms again. "I worried that maybe there was something wrong. I was afraid. But I just kept going because they went away. So I figured I was okay. After all, I was doing what I wanted, what I felt I had to do and had worked so hard for and dreamed of doing. It wasn't going to be easy; it was going to be hard. But I was going to do it and that's all there was to it."

Stubborn and obsessed with his dream, Terry never considered that he was risking his life to pay back his debt and prove he was not disabled. "I was paying the price all the time. If I was running up Burnaby Mountain I was paying the price right there. The pain and the fatigue, the work and the hours, the hours I put into it every day. My life went around my running."

Terry had little time for reflection, or even for running, in the last days before leaving home, although he was still writing notes in his diary exhorting himself to run every day. But he was busy making preparations for the trip and giving local radio, television, and newspaper interviews. He was already used to interviewers. As an amputee who was an accomplished athlete, he had drawn attention and had been the subject of several feature stories. Among those most loyal to Terry early and consistently in his hometown were CJOR radio, CKVU television's evening interview program "The Vancouver Show," and the *Columbian*, the New Westminster daily newspaper.

By the end of the first week of April, Doug and Terry were ready to leave. There was a little crowd at the airport, which included Rika, Doug's parents, Betty, Rolly, Darrell, Judith, Fred and his girlfriend, Theresa, Blair MacKenzie and his two daughters, and Harry Crawshaw and his wife. Crawshaw was the octogenarian who claimed to have set a new record cycling across Canada for the Cancer Society.

Terry shook hands with everyone, including Rika, who wondered why he didn't kiss her goodbye. Then he hugged his dad and Judith, who was crying, and last of all his mother, who was also weeping. He held on to her for the longest time, tried to hold back his own tears, but couldn't. It was difficult for him to leave, not knowing what lay ahead.

As he and Doug strapped themselves into their seats at the front of the Pacific Western Airlines 737, Terry looked up in surprise to see the smiling face of a BCTV reporter with a micro-phone in her hand. Was she going with them? Not at all, it was just the farewell interview.

Terry's journey began in the glare of camera lights, a chorus of goodbyes, loving tears, and the roar of jet engines. He could never have dreamed it then, but when he returned to British Columbia he would be not just a hometown hero; he would be known and admired by nearly everyone in Canada. He'd be spoken of with pride and sorrow.

He had already accomplished something wonderful in train-ing: 3,159.5 miles. The next 5,300 miles would be his gift to cancer patients and all those who needed to believe in miracles. Those next 5,300 would be for us.

7

"I'M TRYING TO RAISE AS MUCH MONEY AS I CAN"

Few are lucky enough to see Canada as Terry did, step by step, mile by mile. Few would know the simple acts of kindness and generosity that were offered to him along the way. Strangers opened their doors, shared their meals with him, gave him a warm bed, and showed they cared about him. He remembered everyone who was kind to him – those pictures of goodness stayed sharp and clear in Terry's mind. As he ran, he passed scenes of ordinary Canadian life played out on the roads. Those images were with him long afterward.

"I remember going through Gander and seeing kids playing road hockey. Where are those kids now? Are they still playing road hockey? Are they playing in a rink? I think about that, all across Canada. What are people doing in the little towns, the people that I met?"

Terry kept a diary of his run. The entries from the early months capture Terry's sense of adventure and the freshness of every new experience. There was despair, too, as he wondered if people understood his message and believed in his dream. He was often frustrated with the Canadian Cancer Society. Support from the society was erratic: he'd raise thousands of dollars in a little town with good organization, then nothing in a city where the society had failed to mobilize its volunteers.

And there were frightening times when he feared for his life as enormous trucks sped by him on the highway. He also wondered if his body could endure the stress of running a marathon, 26 miles, nearly every day. One day he described running as "the usual torture."

NEWFOUNDLAND
April 18, Port Blandford
140 miles

> As we were passing through Port Blandford, Mr. Roland Greening drove by me and told me to come to his store when I was finished. I took a fifteen-minute break and took off again. I was very, very tired and could only manage another two miles. We got just inside the Terra Nova National Park. Back at Mr. Greening's store, Mrs. Greening directed us to the house, which was a beautiful old home right beside the ocean. Here I had a bath and made my phone calls.

Terry learned that Greening had had cancer in his thyroid two years earlier. After they ate their meal, a cheese cod soufflé, which made a big impression on Terry, two girls came by the house and asked if they could see Terry and Doug.

"They were about fifteen, I think. They were shy. They sat down and didn't say anything. Finally I started talking to them and asking them about their school. Then they started asking me a few things. Before they left, they asked me to come over and they both asked if they could have a kiss, so I kissed them both and then they went away.

"About half an hour later, about ten girls came over – those two girls had come back with eight more – and they were all shy again. It was fantastic. I showed them my leg, and how it works, and we joked about not having to change my socks. It was a really warm time. Doug really liked it, too. Then they weren't so shy any more. They became open and I had one of the best times I've ever had. If I could have done that every night it would have been relaxing.

"You know, we all became friends, all these little fifteen-year-old girls. When they left, they all did the same thing. They kissed me."

April 19, Glovertown
165 miles

During my rest period Caleb Ackerman met us. I had an hour's rest and then did another four miles. Those miles were tough until Mr. Ackerman, with his Newfoundland and Canadian flags, came up behind me in his car. Then I breezed through my final couple of miles. We made it just outside the Terra Nova Park. Here I got in the car with Caleb, and he drove us through Glovertown, a-honkin' his horn. We went to a gym where girls were playing basketball. There I was very unprepared to speak, but I told everyone what I was doing and we collected over $100. Caleb phoned ahead to try and increase receptions for us in towns ahead.

April 20, Gambo
190 miles

I find the downhills very jarring on my body. Along the way, two ladies from Clarenville stopped by on their way to Gander, where they were dropping off a lady going to Scotland. They gave me a beautiful old cross as a friendly gesture. I find many people taking my photograph. . . . Then we drove ten miles back to Gambo where we met Gus Barrow. He drove us to the fire hall, where practically the whole town was waiting. It was really beautiful. The mayors of Glovertown and Gambo introduced me and then I talked to the crowd. In fifteen minutes we raised more than $700 in a town with less than 3,000 people. It was a fantastic feeling and a day I will never forget because I hope it is a start of things to come.

April 21, Gander
215 miles

"In Gambo people came and lined up and gave me ten, twenty bucks just like that," he said. "And that's when I knew that the run had unlimited potential. I started to try to do whatever I could to let the Cancer Society know about that potential. I needed them. I tried to let them know as best I could that I was dependent on them to have things prepared and set up before I got there. In some places they did it; in some places, they didn't. It was frustrating for me because I knew there was not only money not being raised but people who I could have inspired, people who could have learned something, were missing me and that was because of the Cancer Society. But in Newfoundland, considering that I was just starting and they had no idea, they didn't know how people were going to respond, just as I didn't. All in all, I'm happy with the Newfoundland Cancer Society. They tried. Theirs is not a wealthy province, and they were the very first one."

His good day in Gambo contrasted with a bad day in Gander:

We drove to Gander city hall where there were three people waiting for us, including the mayor. It was a great disappointment considering the day before in Gambo. We talked to reporters for an hour and then came back to the hotel. I went for a beautiful drive.

April 25, Springdale
312 miles

Sometimes Terry would go for a solitary drive, put on some of the tapes he liked, Hank Williams or Johnny Cash, and go until he found the ocean.

I liked the ocean, but not only that: I liked to drive away, just for the fact of driving, being free and relaxing and listening to music. I remember that free hour when I could just roam. I'd think, Here I am in, Gander, Newfoundland.

Our privacy is starting to be invaded and we can't get anything done. I am happy with the fundraising, but upset that we don't have time to talk and meet people. At night, quite often, people were looking at the van and snooping around. Today the valve system on my leg had completely eroded away and was making a farting noise with every step. I got many sores from this so I had to convert over to my spare leg.

April 26, South Brook Junction
Day 15
337 miles

Today we got up at 4:00 a.m. As usual, it was tough. We drove the thirty-five miles back to the starting point and I took off again. This time I had the other leg with the ordinary knee. I had to consider at the start whether it would be effective. It was foggy this morning so I ran on the left side of the road. We wanted to cover fourteen miles right away because there was going to be a reception at the South Brook

Junction. I was feeling pretty good and the first two and three-quarters miles went quite nicely. Then, all of a sudden, I was seeing eight pictures of everything. I was dizzy and light-headed, but I made it to the van. It was a frightening experience. Was it all over? Was everything finished? Would I let everybody down? Slowly the seeing double went away but my eyes were glassy and I was still light-headed. I told myself it is too late to give up. I would keep going no matter what happened. If I died, I would die happy because I was doing what I wanted to do. How many people could or can say that? I went out and did fifteen pushups in the road and took off. My head was light but the double-sightedness went away. At five miles Doug and I talked about it for a while. I cried because I knew I was going to make it or be in a hospital bed or dead. I want to set an example that will never be forgotten. It is courage and not foolishness. It isn't a waste.

April 29, Deer Lake
412 miles

It was another one of those days when nothing was organized so we raised very little money. Nobody came to meet us in a town of 5,000. I took another break during which I phoned the local schools to let them know I would be coming back tomorrow. Then I did another three miles. I would have liked to have done more but I was drained and we had to meet the mayor at 5:00 p.m. We were given a room at the Deer Lake Hotel and a free meal. After this I showered and made my umpteen millionth phone call. I called Ron Calhoun [special events chairman of the Cancer Society] and had a good conversation. Things will be better from now on, I hope.

When Terry was halfway across Newfoundland, Dr. Robert Macbeth of the National Cancer Institute received the report on Terry's heart. He was worried and arranged a medical examination for Terry in Corner Brook. Terry knew the appointment was scheduled, but skipped it.

May 1, Corner Brook
465 miles

"One Roman Catholic School I will never forget. They sang a song to receive me. Part of the words were: 'Thank you, Lord, for giving us Terry.' It was beautiful, it really brought tears to my eyes."

Terry didn't know it at the time, but the children of All Hallows School donated all their recess money to the Marathon of Hope. He told the children, "I bet some of you feel sorry for me. Well, don't. Having an artificial leg has its advantages. I've broken my right knee several times and it doesn't hurt a bit."

May 3, St. George's Junction
515 miles

I got in the fire truck with a Mr. Tim Conway, who had done a wonderful job in setting everything up. Near the town I got out and walked to the fire hall. The local cadets walked behind me and so did a lot of the townspeople. They played "When the Saints Go Marching In." It was a magnificent feeling. I was really stirred. I raised about $800. Everyone wanted my autograph and a kiss. The reception really picked me up. Then we ate a cold meal and a warm meal at a nearby restaurant and another meal at a gas station. This last one was the first meal we have had to pay for. Then we drove to a hideout and I did my postcards and went to bed.

May 4, past St. George's on Highway 1
521 miles

Today at 4:30 a.m., I couldn't get out of bed. I was sick and
my stomach was in knots. I lay there and later Doug drove to
the starting point. We had a big argument, so we drove back
to a place on the highway and I slept again. But I never got
better. I finally tried to run. It was snowing and miserable,
and I had a huge hill to go up. I couldn't even manage a
hundred yards without standing to hold my stomach and
catch my breath. I managed three miles and then crawled
into the van. I cried so hard and felt so weak. I changed and
slept. I think the problem was something we ate last night.

Later I had some tomato soup and hot chocolate. Then
I went to bed. When I woke up I made myself eat some cake
and had some oranges and some milk. My stomach was still
upset and I was a bit weak, but I felt a bit better.

May 5, on the road to Port aux Basques
548 miles

Today the terrain was up and down. We are passing through
a mountain range. We learned today they had already collected more than $8,000 in Port aux Basques. Fantastic. I
really want to make Port aux Basques tomorrow because
they have got everything planned, but I am worried that I
might not be strong enough to make it. We stayed at the
Starlight Hotel where we were given our meal and lodging.
I had a real good shower here. Then I drove to the ocean.
Newfoundland has two things, the ocean and people. There
is really no scenery or vegetation here.

The next day, the citizens of Port aux Basques, a town with a
population of ten thousand, raised another two thousand

dollars, making their total contribution ten thousand, equal to one dollar per person.

Despite the excitement, optimism, and comparative freedom of the first months, trouble was brewing between Terry and Doug. Doug was sometimes silent, uncommunicative, and Terry was frustrated. Both were stubborn.

"I know I did stuff I shouldn't have," Doug said. "Terry wanted me to make phone calls to arrange publicity and give interviews. I thought he should have made the phone calls. For one thing, nobody wanted to talk to me, they wanted to talk to Terry Fox. If you're calling B.C. from Newfoundland, you might as well put Terry Fox on the line.

"After a while I didn't want to do anything for him, just drive the van, which wasn't nice of me. I think I went too far with pride and rebellion. It wasn't the Christian thing to do. You know sometimes when you do things that they're wrong, but you do them anyhow.

"We'd still be talking but the tension was really bad. Twice I refused to mark miles for him. At Kelly's Mountain, Nova Scotia, he had to throw rocks at the van to get my attention because I was always reading. It was my job to stand by the van at the end of each mile and have water ready for him. Sometimes I would just stretch out my hand to give him his water and neither of us would say a word. Once when I handed him water he just threw it in my face.

"At Grand Falls and Bishop's Falls he agreed to speak to three high schools. The next day he was pissed off and didn't want to do it. I couldn't figure out why he was so mad. There seemed to be a double side. Sometimes he didn't seem to give a damn about other people; at other times he gave an incredible damn. It took me three months to figure out how tough it was. Tougher than any of us could ever know.

"Sometimes I wondered how much was obsession and how much was devotion. After a while I saw there was more devotion than I had figured. It was a fine line he had to balance between keeping in the public eye, keeping the Cancer Society happy, keeping me happy, and accomplishing the run.

"Sometimes he'd bitch at me about a mile marker, that it seemed like a long one. Once it was. The mile ended in the middle of a hill and there was nowhere to pull over, so I went to the top of a hill and he had to run an extra three-quarters of a mile. Boy, was he mad! In Newfoundland I told him I couldn't care less whether he made it or not. Of course, I didn't mean it. But he just made me so mad."

NOVA SCOTIA
May 7, North Sydney
579 miles
Sensing that he had some momentum after the good fundraising experiences in Newfoundland, Terry called the Cancer Society's national office and its Nova Scotia office and told them: "'You've got a lot of potential here. Use me.'" But Nova Scotia did not. We made more money in Newfoundland than we did in Nova Scotia. When we got to Sydney, Nova Scotia, there were two or three people from the Cancer Society waiting for us, and Sydney's a pretty big place. That was pretty upsetting because I'd made it all the way across Newfoundland and now I've made it to Nova Scotia, things were picking up, $10,000 in the little tiny town of Port aux Basques, and here we are in big Sydney and there's nothing, absolutely nothing. Nobody even knew. It wasn't even in the media."

The pressure was mounting on Terry. He was having his troubles with Doug, he had to do the running, and he had to make phone calls to urge the media to cover the run.

"We decided we would go into town and try to get a bunch of media stuff going. We went to all the radio stations and did a lot of work. Since I hadn't slept all night because we had a rough crossing on the ferry from Newfoundland, I was already tired. Then the CBC wanted to film me running, so we decided that I would go out and run again."

A terrifying accident on the highway nearly ended the Marathon of Hope.

"The CBC was filming me from the side, right on the Trans-Canada Highway. They were only going about five miles an hour when I heard this huge freight truck come barrelling up and not slowing down. Smack. At fifty miles per hour it hit the CBC vehicle, forcing it off the road, over a ditch and into the woods. One of the CBC men fell out the back onto the highway and rolled into the ditch. I thought he was dead. He was conscious but couldn't move. The other two guys were hurt, but not seriously. The CBC truck was totalled and the camera equipment ruined. It was terrible. If I had been five yards further ahead, I would have been killed. If the accident had occurred 30 yards before, the two in the truck would have gone down a big ravine. We went to see them in the hospital. I couldn't run any more."

May 10, Port Hawkesbury
660 miles

The Cancer Society here in Nova Scotia is doing nothing and money is being wasted. I would love to get my hands on the people in Halifax. Bob McKeighan from the Ford dealership in Port Hawkesbury came and saw us. He was going to set things up and have dinner with us. He also got our clothes cleaned and the van vacuumed. He is very nice. So is his wife.

May 14, Highway 7
767 miles

Twenty-six miles is now my daily minimum. It is beautiful, quiet, peaceful country. I love it. Very few dogs, so far. Few or no trucks. Very little traffic. I need this. It is nice not to have huge freight trucks ramming past me. I am now carrying my own water bottle when I run and making my own lunches. Doug won't do a thing for me. I saw four rabbits and a beaver today. Also one dead porcupine and two dead skunks. After running I drove up an old road to a big hill in the middle of nowhere. No one can find us here. A peaceful evening, finally. Got lots done. Postcards, shit container cleaned, etc. Made my supper. We were in a field on the top of a hill. Beautiful!

May 15, Sheet Harbour
794 miles

We parked in a beautiful location overlooking the sea. The ocean was much prettier today because of the sunshine. After my break I ran until a lady from the Cancer Society in Sheet Harbour came to see me. They had a reception set up for me at 5:00 and wanted me to run with the school kids. When I ran with the kids I really burned it just to show them how fast I could go. They were tired and puffing. All right! I met quite a few people who had cancer. A great reception, finally, in Nova Scotia. Today I was feeling dizzy and light-headed again.

By mid-May, Terry was finally starting to feel the warm spring sun on his back as he ran. His face was ruddy, windburned, and thinner, and his cheekbones more prominent. His body seemed frailer than when he had left, but he dismissed comments about his weight, saying he had lost only seven pounds, most of that from his upper torso. He had bulked up from weightlifting before he left home; now with the régime of running, it seemed natural that he would lose weight.

In Port Coquitlam, Betty and Rolly watched the evening and late-night news, hoping for a glimpse of their son. Although he called them collect every Thursday and was always upbeat, they wanted to see for themselves that he was well. They were worried by what they saw on television. Betty thought he seemed too thin and worn out. Then Terry called in tears from Sheet Harbour, Nova Scotia, needing their help. He said he was unhappy and desperate. Doug had withdrawn completely and Terry could not cope alone.

Betty and Rolly took a week's vacation and flew to Halifax to see Terry and to try to sort out the problem with Doug. The discussions took place in the house of a "nice little lady who lived somewhere off Highway 7 in Nova Scotia. There was all this swearing," Betty recalled, "and I would have been swearing, too, if I wasn't in that lady's house!"

Betty and Rolly were both fair-minded. It may have been tempting to take Terry's side, but they stood squarely in the middle. They knew that Doug was stubborn, just as Terry was. They knew that Terry was demanding and that Doug would withdraw rather than stand up to him. They encouraged Doug to say what was on his mind and used the example of newlyweds who had to learn to get along together in close quarters.

"If you have to yell, yell," Betty told Doug.

Terry said his parents straightened them out. "They showed me how to understand Doug's side more, and I think Doug saw my side more. Just having them to talk to as a go-between was important and good. You see, all along I never had anybody to talk to. When I was frustrated I was alone. Doug was somebody

I couldn't talk to. We worked under pressure. I realized I was hurting him at times, that I was bitching too much at times. Doug realized that he could help me more, too."

A few days later, Terry tried to let Doug know that he valued him in an emotional speech at the Dartmouth Vocational School.

May 20, Dartmouth
916 miles

With my parents we took the ferry across the bay and met the mayor of Dartmouth. Then I ran to the vocational school here with fifty students. I ran about a mile. They had raised about $3,000. What a great group of kids! Too bad not everybody was doing that. I did my speech and I couldn't help but cry when I said how Doug had to have courage to put up with and understand me when I'm tired and irritable. Then we drove back to Truro.

Had supper with my parents. A lady gave me a picture of her daughter and told me to phone her and that she liked me.

Terry told the Halifax *Mail Star* that day: "[People] seem to forget what I am doing this for. They think I am running across Canada on some kind of ego trip. It is a personal challenge, but I'm trying to raise as much money as I can. . . . I need their support."

May 22, Springhill
972 miles

It poured rain for the last two miles. Thunderstorm and lightning. My mom and dad came out for the last five miles. After that we drove to Springhill, where we met Ron Jefferson, who had done a fantastic job organizing things here. I was in a bitchy mood, unfortunately. I wish I could relax more. Anyway, I ran another mile into city hall with fire engines and a police escort. There were a lot of people here to meet me. I did my speech and it went well and then I signed autographs. After that we went for a lobster dinner (great) with Ron and some other firemen and my parents. We learned about the mine explosion here and that Anne Murray was from here. After that we came to a boarding house to sleep. They gave me some good advice. Be disappointed in the fundraising, but not mad! I've got to try to control myself. My mom and dad left tonight for an early flight tomorrow morning.

PRINCE EDWARD ISLAND
May 24, Borden
1,028 miles

I made it perfectly for the 2:30 p.m. ferry across Northumberland Strait to Prince Edward Island. We met the captain on board and he spent about an hour with us. It was great. Then I ran four and a quarter miles into Borden. It was a cute town. I had a very heavy wind in my face. Then we went to a motel where we met people from the Cancer Society in Charlottetown who are doing a fabulous job. I had a great shower and watched part of the sixth game of the Stanley Cup playoffs between Philly and the New York Islanders. Then I drove to Summerside. It is beautiful country. I finally relaxed!

May 25, Highway 1 to Charlottetown
1,056 miles

Today I made it out of bed again. Boy, was it a beautiful morning. In terms of sun, weather, and terrain this was the most beautiful day so far. A guy from the local radio station was actually there at 5:00 in the morning when we took off. He covered us all day. What a tremendous support! The first twelve miles were relaxing. We parked right on the ocean, away from everything. Great!

When we went back out it was cloudy, windy, and cold. The next ten miles were okay. I was in some hilly areas, still beautiful. There were lots of people out to cheer me on and support me. Incredible! We collected over $600 on the road today, our best. We also learned that they now have $40,000 in Newfoundland. I was very sore and tired. It is hard to even walk. I've got to get up and over the pain threshold. When I came out of the van after my rest I was weary, but there was a long line of cars and people to cheer me on so l made it. I had another dizzy spell during the run. Still freezing, but I wasn't wearing sweats so people could see my leg. I'd run just over twenty-eight miles.

Terry doesn't make note of it in his diary, but by now he had overcome his shyness and nervousness in talking before crowds. It had become almost second nature to him.

May 26, Charlottetown
1,074 miles

I was scheduled to run into Charlottetown at 9:00 a.m. Therefore I got a chance to sleep in. It was great! We got up at 7:00 a.m. I did some postcards. We had to drive to a school where I talked to 900 kids. Boy, were they ever a happy group. Then I ran three miles into town. Along the way, two schools greeted me and cheered me on. Many people are congratulating me and I can't figure out what for.

Early in the morning, Doug recalled, a tiny woman came out of her house and walked down the road to the van. She was wearing her nightgown and slippers and had a five-dollar bill in her hand. She asked if anybody wanted coffee, then went back into her house.

NEW BRUNSWICK
May 28, 28 miles, Moncton
1,130 miles

The springs in my knee joint are worn away but I struggled and pounded out the twelve miles. I saw a moose. We went back to Shediac High School where I talked to about 900 students. They were all Acadians. I really enjoyed these people. Around five people fainted during the speech. It was very hard to believe! Then we went out to talk to more media and Stan Barker of the Cancer Society took my leg to Fredericton to get it repaired. I put on the other leg and it was worse. After a half-mile I fell flat on my face. I couldn't keep my balance and I was struggling to make ground again. My foot and leg and back are all being overstressed to compensate for the malfunctioning knee joint. I didn't think I would make it twenty-eight miles, but I did and it was fantastic when I made it. I couldn't believe I was looking at the back of the van for the last time that day. We ran right through the city of Moncton, down the main street, and collected a lot of money. When one car would start to honk, they all would! It was great.

The next day was the kind that frustrated Terry more than he could express. The worst was having to drive a hundred miles round trip back to Moncton to attend a press conference and a fundraising dinner after slogging twenty-nine miles through heat and humidity. He hadn't slept the night before –

coming from British Columbia, he wasn't used to the muggy atmosphere.

May 29, 29 miles, Highway 2, west of Moncton
1,159 miles

> I was dead all morning for twelve miles. For the next ten miles, the paved shoulder on the Trans-Canada had a steep slant and it is hard on my ankle. I took another break, during which I made phone calls, and then did my last seven miles. We drove back fifty miles to Moncton and later we drove fifty miles back to bed. We learned that Saint John would have nothing organized for us. I can't believe it.
>
> We were advised to go directly on the Trans-Canada #2 (and bypass Saint John). I try so hard and then get let down. I am going to run right down this city's main street. Doug is going to follow behind and honk. We will be rebels, we will stir up noise. People will know Terry Fox ran out of his way to Saint John for a reason!

Terry's brother Darrell, who was seventeen at the time, wrote his high-school finals early, missed his graduation, and joined the Marathon of Hope in Saint John. The family hoped Darrell, with his sparky humour and good nature, would be a buffer between Terry and Doug.

For Darrell, it was the start of the proudest three months of his life. He felt connected with history in the making. His jokes and sly tricks may have obscured what was otherwise obvious: he admired and adored his big brother.

It wasn't long before Darrell would be asked how he felt about Terry. Was Terry in any way the typical cloddish older brother, broadcaster Jeremy Brown wondered? "He's my idol," Darrell answered. "I respect him in every way. We fight a lot, which could be expected, but we love each other a lot."

May 31, 29 miles, Saint John
1,217 miles

> I was still sore all day. The first twelve miles were awful, especially the final three during which I was dead tired. Also pissed off that nothing was being done in Saint John.
>
> Fortunately, the mayor, who is a heart-attack victim and a marathon runner, got a radio station behind me and the local paper. The next ten miles were better. Darrell arrived and it was very heartwarming to see him. Brought a few tears as we embraced. Got me moving a bit faster. We finished right in the middle of Saint John.

According to a Cancer Society internal memo, Terry refused a medical in New Brunswick. His parents indicated that he was old enough to make his own decisions and they were not about to influence him. Betty said it didn't happen that way. "What we said was that if we, as parents, had had any say, Terry never would have started."

Darrell was devoted to Terry and couldn't wait to swing into the rhythm of the Marathon of Hope. "By the time I got there," Darrell said, "things seemed okay between Terry and Doug. They seemed to have settled down. I didn't notice anything wrong. The first few days I just watched. I didn't know how things worked. I'd see how they did things and then I'd help.

"When I first saw Terry on the highway, he looked so lonely. Just to look at the road, to see it keep going, even each bend is so long. I don't know why, but I hugged him, I couldn't help myself. In the middle of Saint John, the cars went by. People just looked at him in amazement. They'd just stare. They didn't know what was going on. I was mad when he ran through the city and there was nobody; to go out of his way and raise nothing, it was a complete waste of time. All that work for nothing. It seemed that Stan Barker of the Cancer Society was the only one doing anything.

"There were a lot of firsts for me. To be given free meals and to give interviews, all that was new. Then later, I saw the way Terry affected people. Once he was talking at a baseball game; everyone looked so interested and clapped for him, and the players came out to shake his hand. Sometimes it didn't seem like there was much to be done – just give Terry support, tell him how good he looked running."

June 1, 23 miles, Highway 7
1,240 miles

> It's really good to have Darrell along. It was boiling hot and I got very tired and the miles went slowly. One idiot tried to drive me off the road. I took my break and tried again, but only managed one mile. I am very tired and sore. I need a break and I've got to take it. I'll turn failure to victory.
>
> Goal: Home October 31st. Miles to go: 4,060 out of total 5,300. Twenty-eight miles a day! 145 running days to October 31st. 153 days left till October 31st. Therefore eight days to spare.

June 6, 30 miles, Bristol
1,376 miles

> Today it was a beautiful morning. No wind, sunny, and the sun coming up was great. Beautiful farmland. The first few miles were the usual torture. My foot was blistered bad, but my stump wasn't too bad. After twelve miles I found out we had to drive back to Hartland and meet the mayor. The mayor wasn't there so I went to a school and talked to a large group of kids. Then, exhausted, I slept. Today I had tremendous support. Everybody honked and waved.

People all over looked out of their homes and stores and cheered me on.

June 7, 26 miles, Perth-Andover
1,402 miles

I was in pain this morning and continually stopped to relieve the pressure. Slowly but surely twelve miles went by and left me just out of Perth-Andover. We parked in a beautiful grass field along the Saint John River. On my mile twelve, a guy told me to look for a young bull moose in a pond, but I saw a deer. I slept very well while Doug and Darrell read on the riverbank. Later in the town there was tremendous support and it quickened my pace right up for the remaining fourteen miles. I flew!

Terry ran his all-time high of thirty miles per day in this period. Doug was worried when he ran that far every day, "because he had to run those miles, go to those receptions, and there seemed no way he could do it. He was at his limit, absolutely all out all day. There was not a moment for him to relax."

In Edmundston, cheery, plump Bill Vigars from the Ontario division of the Cancer Society joined the Marathon of Hope briefly to meet Terry, learn his schedule, and prepare them for what he was certain would be the big-top performance that awaited them in Ontario. Vigars had a sense of vision, could spin a good story, thought big, and had the energy to get things done. Who did Terry want to meet? Movie stars? Television celebrities? Terry told him he wanted to meet Bobby Orr and Darryl Sittler. Vigars was exactly what Terry and Doug needed.

Doug, who was usually the first one up in the morning, remembered taking the gear out to the van at 4:30. There was Vigars, sleeping in his car outside their hotel, having driven all night from Toronto. It was their first meeting.

"I was getting the van ready and this guy jumps out; he's just putting his shirt on. I couldn't believe this was the Bill Vigars I had been talking to on the phone. I expected a man with a suit and a tie, and here was chubby little Bill, about thirty, with glasses.

"He was talking about a Toronto Blue Jays baseball game, about meeting Darryl Sittler, Bobby Orr, what they were going to do. We had high expectations. I'd told Bill on the phone that our goal in Ontario was a million dollars. He'd sort of laughed, but he was really interested in getting things done. Bill really believed it would be big – ten million dollars anyway.

"It was high-class. They had everything organized, the centre of Canada, it was like something great was going to happen." But first Terry had to run through Quebec, where no one knew who he was, where he raised little money, and where drivers tried to force him off the road.

QUEBEC
June 10, 30 miles, Notre-Dame-du-Lac
1,482 miles

> Today I felt quite good at the start; the only problem is my cysts are bothering me. The first nine miles took me to the Quebec–New Brunswick border. Here we said goodbye to Stan [Barker], and also to Bill Vigars for a while. The wind picked up and was hard in my face. We learned that there would be very little done in Quebec. Apparently they can't speak English. Maybe they also don't get cancer.

June 11, 26 miles, Highway 185
1,508 miles

> We slept well last night. It was quite cold in the van. The wind howled again all day. Right in my face. It is very difficult constantly running into the wind. It zaps it right out of

your body and head. The first twelve miles were good and
bad, off and on. Very hilly country all day. Lots of forest. All
forest! My stump is still constantly giving me trouble. We
parked down by a lake. All alone in the woods. Can't wash or
shave or get a haircut. The only people here who know about
the run are the truckers and the out-of-province people.
Everyone else wants to stop and give me a lift.

June 12, 27 miles, Andréville
1,535 miles

The St. Lawrence River is beautiful, so large. This is the best
scenery we have had. The towns are simply gorgeous. We
made it to St. André [Andréville]. Here we phoned and
camped behind the school for the night.

None of the trio of West Coast boys could speak French. Doug
made an effort to say he couldn't speak French, the others could say
no more than *oui* and *non*. In grocery stores, they'd point at what
they wanted. They couldn't figure out how to ask for a shower, so
they did without. "I felt like an idiot, an alien from another planet,"
Doug recalled, "so we went four or five days without a wash."

Friday, June 13, 24 miles, Highway 20
1,559 miles

The wind is simply howling and shaking. It is terrible. No
way could I run against it, so I had to run behind the van. It
was hard on Doug trying to stay a distance away. Terrible,
ugly day. Somehow we turned zero miles into twenty-four. I
got sick from the exhaust fumes of the van. I was given a
beautiful shower and I was so dirty. Felt good!

Darrell, in the back of the van, sat with his left leg stretched out
to keep the one side of the door open and his right arm stretched

the other way to keep the right door open to protect Terry from the wind. The tape deck was turned on high, as they listened to old rock and roll songs from *American Graffiti.*

"I'd look into Terry's eyes," Darrell said. "It was like he was looking at nothing, like he was chasing the van, like he was going to hop on for a ride. It hurt having to watch him suffering. He'd run by a pole and I'd watch it get farther and farther away, then another would take its place. He wouldn't look at me so I'd watch his face a lot. He had to wear a jacket, the wind was blowing so hard. I watched it blowing his curls back from his face."

June 15, 26 miles, Highway 20
1,611 miles

> I am tired and weary because people are continually forcing me off the road. I was actually honked off once. People are passing from behind me on this narrow road. It is so frustrating. They all drive at eighty miles per hour and don't slow down for anything. It is wearisome. Mental breakdown. We talked and ate with John Simpson and Scott Hamilton [filmmakers working on the Cancer Society–sponsored documentary, *I Had a Dream*] and then I did a long interview. In bed late again.

Terry thought Quebec was beautiful. He admired the statues around the churches, the cobbled streets and the tidy, antiquated shops of old Quebec City. He saw the battlefield on the Plains of Abraham, and it was fun to eat in a restaurant named the Marie Antoinette. He met Gérard Côté, four-time Boston Marathon winner (1940, 1942, 1943, and 1948), and was happy to be featured on the front page of the French-language daily, *Le Soleil.* That was all very nice, but he wasn't raising money, running conditions were dangerous, and he wasn't meeting many people. He believed if the marathon had been better publicized, Quebecers would have responded as other Canadians had.

"It was very disappointing; it's not because they're French and we're English. Anyone can get cancer. I'm running across Canada, and Quebec is a province in Canada. With me, it isn't a political or racial thing, it's just a human thing. Cancer can strike anybody. I'm trying to help out everybody in my run. In one stretch of Quebec, we collected thirty-five dollars while I ran one hundred miles."

Nor was he helped by the attitude of motorists and the police: "Near Quebec City I kept nearly getting hit because they drove so fast. Afterwards I decided I had to move over to the freeway, which had a side lane. It was perfectly safe and nobody was near me. I ran there for two days when the Quebec Provincial Police told me I couldn't run on it any more because it wasn't safe [and because of the traffic expected for the St-Jean-Baptiste holiday weekend]. I had to get back on these other side roads. In Drummondville I got back on the little roads and kept nearly getting hit again. These cars were just whizzing by and shooing me off the road."

Then Terry learned that he would have to wait in Montreal so he would arrive in Ottawa for Canada Day celebrations, in accordance with the schedule set up by Bill Vigars. He agreed only when Bill told him the difference it might mean in fundraising.

Terry ran into Montreal on a Sunday, using a route he had chosen and mapped out himself. He was accompanied by four wheelchair athletes and former Montreal Alouettes kicker Don Sweet. As he and the others ran down the quiet morning streets, there were few passersby to cheer him on.

He was running to the luxurious Four Seasons Hotel, where they would be pampered as guests of the international hotel chain's president, Isadore Sharp. Sharp, who was a devoted phi-lanthropist, had lost his teenage son, Chris, to cancer. He felt a connection with Betty and Rolly. "I knew what they were going through, the sense of hopelessness that comes with this dreaded disease. There is no feeling more difficult to deal with than that, and talking to Betty Fox, I could hear the pain in her voice."

Along with some of his business partners, he decided to challenge the corporate community to raise money for the Marathon of Hope. He took out full-page newspaper ads with the slogan "Let's make Terry's run really count," saying that the Four Seasons was donating two dollars for every mile Terry would run, and challenged 999 corporations to do the same.

Terry, Doug, and Darrell didn't quite know what to make of the elegant surroundings, although Terry stood under a shower for an hour – or so he said. The night before, they'd stayed in a convent, each in a tiny cell, a contrast to the comfort of the hotel where each was given his own suite. "I'm not used to seeing luxurious things," Darrell said later. "Our laundry bill was eighty dollars. Our T-shirts came back from the cleaners with paper around them, like when you buy them brand new!" Darrell was proud of those Marathon of Hope shirts, because his name was printed on the back identifying him as Terry's brother.

One night, while Darrell was collapsed in front of a television set that wasn't working properly, Bev Norris, a Four Seasons publicist, walked in the room. She watched in amazement as Darrell got up and pounded the set.

"Darrell Fox," Bev said in a mock-schoolteacher tone, "do you realize you're staying in a three-hundred-dollar-a-night room?"

"How much would it cost if the TV worked?" Darrell shot back, grinning.

On June 23, Terry took the day off, and for the first time in seventy-three days of running, he wrote "zero" beside the mileage he recorded in his diary.

Terry was meant to relax in Montreal. He did his best, but it was difficult for him. He didn't like sitting around. He told the *Toronto Star* in an interview that it made him edgy. In fact, relaxation didn't vitalize him, but made him only more anxious to run. He tried to have a good time. He spent some time with an old high-school buddy, Clay Gamble, visited his Uncle Brian, took the subway to see the Olympic Stadium, and watched the Canadian Open Golf Tournament. Doug believed that changing the pace undermined Terry psychologically and threw him off his rhythm.

Once he was on the road again, Terry was dodging cars that zoomed past him at furious speeds. He ran looking over his shoulder. The temperature soared to thirty-two degrees Celsius. The boys started counting the days until they could leave Quebec and the isolation caused by their language difficulties.

8

"IT'S CERTAINLY GREAT TO
GET TO ONTARIO"

I n mid-April, when Terry started running in Newfoundland, few people in Ontario paid attention to him. He had his supporters in British Columbia, but there was a vast distance in between.

Terry's name came up in the weekly features meeting at the *Toronto Star*, Canada's largest newspaper, but there was little interest in following a one-legged runner with a dream.

But something about Terry's story appealed to Bonnie Cornell, editor of the paper's "Family" section. She couldn't get the televised image of the hopeful young man dipping his leg in the Atlantic Ocean out of her mind. She was thinking of her mother, too, who had recently died of cancer of the liver. Cornell was a tough editor with a gift for spotting trends and news stories. Sometimes she bucked the scepticism of the newsroom. In this case, she assigned a reporter to do a feature story on Terry for her section. "Find out if he's for real," Cornell told me.

The *Toronto Star*'s telephone operators have voices soft as honey, but they are cunning as detectives in finding anyone, anywhere in the world. They track their quarry like hunters and their skill is legendary. When I asked them to find a one-legged runner somewhere in Newfoundland, they did so in a few hours. By mid-afternoon the call came through: "We have Mr. Terry Fox on the line."

They had found Terry in the home of the mayor of Come By Chance, Newfoundland. He told his story simply: how he had beaten cancer, how he dreamed of running 5,300 miles and raising money for research, and how he didn't see himself as disabled. He sounded young, happy, hopeful, and excited about what he was doing. He was straightforward and so convincing I didn't hesitate to tell Cornell that, yes, he was for real. And yes, I thought, he is going to run across Canada.

Terry agreed to phone me every week until he reached British Columbia. British Columbia? He had been in Newfoundland less than a week and had run only ninety-two miles, yet I knew I wanted to be in that crowd waiting for him at the ocean on the other side of the country.

I don't know who was more excited. For Terry, it was important to have an influential paper reporting on his run and printing weekly progress reports. And I knew I had been given a great story.

Sometimes it seemed only I thought so. With each weekly report came wisecracks from the newsroom: "How much longer is he going to be hopping across Canada?" "No one ever reads this, you know. It's boring." "It won't be news as long as he runs; it'll only be news when he stops."

Terry and I built up a trust during those early telephone conversations, and our interviews became the highlight of my week. I was disappointed if he was too busy to talk to me himself. When Doug told me that sometimes I worried too much on the telephone and that Terry liked people to be buoyant and positive, I tried to change my tone.

He told me about his dream of ending the run in Stanley Park and how he would raise his arms and dance in the waves, saying to himself, "I did it. I did it!"

Once he told me of the ecstatic heights he reached while running, when his concentration and stride were in harmony and the pain seemed to dissolve: "When I'm really tired, I'm actually crying on the road. I get so emotional, but being in that state keeps me going."

Another day he read part of a poem, "It Couldn't Be Done" by Edgar Albert Guest, that a Nova Scotia admirer, named Mrs. Fox, had given him. He kept the poem tacked on the van's wall and he read it every night before bed.

Sometimes I'd share bits of news that Terry hadn't heard yet: that a song called "Run, Terry, Run," written by Vern Kennedy, had been recorded in his honour, with all royalties going to the Cancer Society; that an anonymous Toronto woman had donated five thousand dollars; and the big news, that Isadore Sharp of the Four Seasons had issued his corporate challenge.

We didn't meet until the last Saturday in June, when the *Star* sent me to Hawkesbury, a francophone town on the edge of the Ottawa River, to cover Terry's arrival in Ontario.

The flashing lights of the van and a police cruiser told me that Terry was nearby, on the Quebec side of the Perley Bridge. I drove ahead to get a sense of what he looked like running.

Anyone who saw Terry run remembers the shock of that first moment. His jaw was clenched, and his face was a grimace, not so much of pain as of concentration. His eyes seemed closed, perhaps to the glare, perhaps to the distractions on the roadside.

As I drove by, I waved, and was surprised to find that I shouted, "Go, Terry!" He didn't look across, but his hand shot up automatically. He was watching the road, and he lurched ahead, shoulders hunched, his body surging forward with the swing of his artificial leg. And he was running – every step demanded effort and energy. I had expected someone bigger and stronger-looking. Although he was five-foot-ten, he seemed small, certainly smaller than he appeared in news photographs. Did he seem that way because he was alone on the highway and that highway, I knew, stretched for thousands more miles? The scene took your breath away. You didn't feel pity. You had to admire his crazy courage, stamina, and conviction. But there was something beautiful here, too, something majestic in the human spirit, to drive him across this vast country, step by aching step.

Back on the Ontario side of the bridge a crowd had formed in front of a little community centre not far from the ball field and the river. A couple of station wagons were parked on the grass. They were filled with printed balloons that read: WELCOME, TERRY. YOU CAN DO IT.

A brass band rehearsed a melody that had a mind of its own. At last Terry was in sight and this time he was flanked by flag-bearers, a couple of men in jogging shorts. The young musicians gathered their courage and their instruments and burst, off-key, into "Georgie Girl." The doors of the station wagons were flung open, and thousands of balloons drifted skyward. The crowd, perhaps two hundred or more, shouted "Hip, hip, hooray!" three times.

Terry walked up the steps of the community centre and shook hands with officials waiting there. The local M.P.P., Albert Bélanger, representing Ontario's Premier Bill Davis, started the ceremonies: "I hope this walk – excuse me, this run . . ." Terry smiled, as he wiped the perspiration from his chin. He rested his hands on his hips, stood a little lopsidedly, and listened.

Terry, the boy too shy to take a university class that required an oral report, took the microphone and told his story. He spoke easily. "It's certainly great to get to Ontario, I'll tell you that. I'm glad you all came out. It makes a difference." Then he spoke of cancer, saying nobody was immune to it, "nobody here, nobody in Hawkesbury." Then he thanked the Cancer Society: "They're taking a chance on me and I think it's going to work out."

As he spoke, the people of Hawkesbury, some of them fresh from the baseball diamond, most of them standing in family groups, stared at the grass. The little children who had snuck up front squatted down and squinted up at Terry.

Then the band started to play and Terry walked inside the community centre for a press conference. As local reporters gathered around him at a table, I stood to the side listening to the questions and watching Terry. His hair, bleached white at the temples, was still damp. His eyebrows had gone the same pale colour, and there were slashes of sunburn on his cheeks. His T-shirt read TERRY FOX, MARATHON OF HOPE, and there was a spot of perspiration, seeping from the valve in his artificial leg, on his grey shorts – the only kind he wore because they bore no logos.

One of the reporters asked if he was running to find himself. The answer came back swiftly, almost defensively: "This isn't soul-searching. I'm not trying to find something. I've found what I want."

Outside, the little fellows from the peewee baseball team, the Fournier Mets, were still milling around. They'd collected six dollars for Terry. They had been too shy to talk to him at the presentation, but now they wanted to watch him run some more.

Fourteen-year-old Charles Tuttle was riding his bike across the grass, doing wheelies, until Terry came out. "I found that story of his very touching," Charles said. "It makes a funny feeling inside me."

I still hadn't introduced myself to Terry, so I went back to the centre where the interviews had wound down and found Terry chatting and shaking hands with well-wishers. I joined the line-up and gave my name, and felt as shy as the Fournier Mets. He apologized for not greeting me sooner. We agreed to talk later and I started looking for Doug and Darrell, who were on the road with the van.

Later, I hopped in the back of the van and for the next thirty-six hours became part of the Marathon of Hope. Terry was already running and was nearly out of sight. He ran into the middle of Hawkesbury's main street, on a busy Saturday afternoon, knowing that the Ontario Provincial Police cruiser and the van had to catch up to him. The OPP were going to follow Terry across Ontario. It was protection his family appreciated as much as Terry did: now he didn't have to check over his shoulder while running.

Although Doug and Darrell had cleaned the van for my benefit, there was still a strong odour from the chemical toilet. I had thought the smell was a combination of food without refrigeration, sweaty socks and T-shirts. Doug and Darrell, who were used to the smell, didn't know the effect it had on visitors.

Terry was to run only nine more miles that day. In fact, when he crossed the Perley Bridge, it was not his first entry into Ontario. He wasn't expected at the bridge until noon and so, rather than waste a morning, they had gotten up at 4:30, when reporters and politicians were still in their beds, and Terry had run ten miles into the province. They marked the distance, then drove back to Quebec, rested, and ran the official first nine miles across the border.

In town, shoppers paused, open-mouthed, their arms full of groceries, as they watched Terry run by. We caught up with him on the outskirts of the town to see him disappear into what seemed a large factory with the OPP officer right behind him. Doug deduced it was a washroom stop, and he was right.

The next seven or so miles were open road. Darrell, who was making preparations for Terry's drink break, noticed they were low on ice – ice that was to be used only for Terry's drinking water. The others drank their soft drinks warm.

I offered to run into a gas station. The proprietress told me, flatly, no ice. Then she realized I was about to return to the van marked TERRY FOX, MARATHON OF HOPE. She stopped me and said, "Wait. Is it for Terry?" I told her it was and she said, "Yes, of course, we can give you ice for Terry. We don't have very much, but please take this."

At the next mile marker Terry stopped for a drink. Darrell hurried to have it waiting for him. He also examined the cup to make sure there was no dirt floating with the ice. Terry was fussy. Darrell asked if he wanted gum, cookies, an orange, and had them all at hand so that he could reach them quickly. Both Darrell and Doug did their jobs quietly. You didn't make small talk with Terry on his breaks.

This was an unexpected intensity. On the telephone, Terry was eager and friendly; here, nothing could interfere with his concentration. It seemed he was protected by an invisible wall. While he was running, no one, nothing, penetrated the barrier. Later Terry explained what his expectations were and why he wanted everything to run smoothly and be predictable, down to the expectation that his cup of water would be clean. "I wanted things to be as comfortable as they could for me when I wasn't running because I was out there, twenty-six miles a day. The moments that I wasn't running were precious to me and I wanted the other guys to realize that.

"We had a routine, Doug and I, and if something wasn't ready when I came in for my break, we would argue a little bit. There may have been tension, but I didn't feel it the way you did. When you were in the van, I had to pretend you weren't there. Things had to be constant. You know when you've done one mile that the next mile's going to be the same, non-changing, and you can do it again. When things interfere – when something happens on this mile that didn't happen before – it breaks your concentration.

"It was like I had to be alone. It had to be like it was when I was training all by myself at home. I didn't need people around me then. I didn't need the water and I didn't need this or that. I could train by myself at home and I needed the same thing when I was running across Canada. I needed to make the same kind of atmosphere.

"When things changed and new things happened, when new people were around, sometimes it really upset me. When I got in the van and things weren't the same, it made it harder."

The week before Terry ran into Ontario, Bill Vigars was at a meeting of the Ontario division of the Cancer Society in a Toronto hotel, where the heads of the regional units were still discussing how they would support Terry on his run. The Toronto and Hamilton units, the two largest, didn't want to ask their volunteers to start up again so soon after the April fundraising season. Vigars waited outside, his bags in hand, ready to join Terry, while the discussion continued. Most were in favour, and some argued passionately on Terry's behalf. Vigars was told to go.

The Marathon of Hope had been offered rooms at the Poplar Motel on Highway 17, a row of low, whitewashed bungalows, with metal lawn chairs outside each door. Terry's room was free, the others were given a five-dollar discount. The motel-keeper, a burly, dark-haired man wearing a cook's apron, came out drying his hands, and solemnly reached for Terry's. "Sir," he said, "it's a pleasure to meet you."

Darrell invited me to chat with Terry while he had a snack. I ordered tea, Terry ordered a cheeseburger, a plate of French fries, a generous slice of apple pie, and a chocolate milkshake. Dinner would come later. We talked about cancer, about how he had never wanted anyone in his family to see him when he was sick. Darrell teased him about the time he'd seen him in the shower without the wig. We talked about running: "People talk about the loneliness of the long-distance runner," Terry said, "but I never feel that. I like to be alone."

Terry agreed to pose for a few photographs, so we sat in the grass in front of the motel while the camera clicked. *Toronto Star* readers wanted to know more about him, and I had a few letters for Terry from them.

These were Terry's precious moments of relaxation. But he didn't have them for long. A Cancer Society representative came up to tell him he was expected to speak at a fair in Plantagenet, just down the road. The protective barrier dropped into place again. The muscles in his cheek tightened. You could feel his anger rise.

"Why wasn't I told before?"

Silence.

"I'm not going." His cheek tightened again.

They told him the mayor was waiting for him, people were passing the hat. It wouldn't take long, but he would have to run into the fair.

"It makes me feel so guilty when I say no," he said as he got up.

He told Doug to drop him just at the crest of a hill leading to the village, whose main feature was a huge church with a silver spire. Terry stepped wearily out of the van and told Darrell to mark the two hundred yards down the hill. He didn't want to have to run them again in the morning. With a good show of speed, he ran into the village and was welcomed by the mayor, who wore a cowboy hat and called to the crowd in French with a loud-hailer.

Terry quickly got to the point: "Any of you could get cancer. I could get it again." Then he signed autographs.

Glowing young girls in pink T-shirts, all blond hair and giggles, shyly approached him with their pens and paper; a pensioner, creaky on his feet, wearing a suit jacket and hat despite the heat, dropped a ten-dollar bill in the collection box and gave Terry a robust handshake. Terry showed the same interest in the pensioner that he had shown in the young girls. He was polite to everyone.

Doug, Darrell, and Terry were quiet on the way back to the motel. It had been a long, hot day. Darrell, slumped against the car seat, finally said, "I'm thinking about what just happened. What the effect of all that will be, what those little kids who saw Terry will do. It's all for the future."

The tidy green farmland, lush with summer's crop, rolled by, and the Marathon of Hope drove silently to its home for the night.

Later, Darrell called me away from my notebook for dinner. Terry ate twice as much as anyone else: a huge steak, a plate of French fries, vegetables, a couple of Cokes. Doug had a plain hamburger. They joked that Doug could live on Terry's leftovers. Terry was animated at the other end of the table, chatting to Cancer Society volunteers. He asked about Quebec and the recent referendum; he was intelligent and curious. He listened well and insisted that Quebec was part of Canada despite its language and cultural differences.

The motel owners fussed over Terry. They brought him a towering strawberry parfait and pointed out a family sitting nearby who were eating there so they could meet Terry. The family came over to shake his hand. It was easy and comfortable. Then, without a word of farewell, he was gone. It was bedtime and scarcely 7:00 p.m. I watched in surprise as he picked up his bag, walked into his room, and drew the drapes.

It was still hours before my bedtime, and I was struck with that fear reporters have when they may have lost a chance for an interview. I looked at Terry's closed door and wondered if I should disturb him during his quiet time. I walked past the door a few times and then into my own room.

At 4:00 the next morning I was awake and dressed and sitting outside in the steel lawn chair waiting for the others to stir. Doug was the first one out. He knocked on Terry's door. A CBC television crew arrived. They trained their brilliant camera lights on Terry's door – a spotlight in the still, black night. At 4:30 he opened his door slowly and walked into the glare, shielding his eyes for only a moment.

I wasn't sure where to sit in the van – the back where Terry was lying down seemed too close. He told me to sit in the front passenger seat. We drove again in silence. The moon was still high and full. A bank of clouds was reflected in the moonlight and skirted the horizon. Grain silos gleamed in the light. Cattle moved uneasily as we sped by.

Terry lay in the back, wrapped in a soft blue sleeping bag, protected, as in a cocoon. He was thinking, he later told me, that he wished it would take an hour to drive to the spot where he was to start running. Darrell was by his side, looking for the pile of rocks by the roadside that marked the previous day's last mile. Sometimes they used rocks, sometimes a piece of paper.

Darrell wondered why they never came up with a more sophisticated way to mark Terry's miles. A couple of times they couldn't find the marker and had to drive back to a spot Terry was certain he had run before he would start again. "It wasn't good enough for me to remember; he had to remember it," Darrell said.

Within a few minutes we left him alone on the road and drove ahead exactly one mile.

I stood on the side of the road to wait for him. The sky was still black. There was silence, and the sweet morning smell of good farmland was all around us. The moon cast the only light. It was Terry's favourite time of day. There were no cars, the temperature was cool, there was no wind. No distractions, no crowds. No speeches. Just Terry doing what he loved doing – running.

He remembered that morning, too: "Some days it was so hard to get going, sometimes it was all pain. I didn't run quickly that morning. I didn't set any speed records, but the miles went so lightly. Right away, that day, they went easily. I just floated. All of a sudden, a mile had gone by."

At dawn, Terry was interviewed by a CBC reporter who wired him for sound and then jogged beside him, asking questions as they went. He had told the reporter he didn't think he'd be able to run and answer questions at the same time, but he accepted it as an interesting challenge and loved it.

Those early miles took thirteen minutes each, compared to his average fourteen-minute miles. By 6:05 a.m. he'd run five miles, and the boys congratulated themselves on their earliest five-mile finish in a long time. In the van, Darrell treated me to a sampler of some Terry's favourite music, including Hank Williams's "Your Cheatin' Heart" and "Jambalaya," while Terry ran. The sun was up, and Terry was beginning to feel its heat. Perspiration had gathered on his chin. At his water break he didn't say a word. He smiled once, just as he set out again, and it was like the sunrise.

Back on the road again, a herd of heifers stopped grazing by the fence and started loping with Terry as he ran past, but he didn't notice.

About 8:00 a.m. Terry took his first morning break while Doug prepared breakfast. He made Terry two peanut butter and honey sandwiches on brown bread, gave him a bowl of beans – for energy – a bowl of Cap'n Crunch cereal, and a couple of Cokes.

The rest of us would find a restaurant later. I chatted with Terry as he ate and once again he was friendly and easy to talk to. There was not even a trace of the intensity that was so intimidating. Those psychological walls he built around himself that allowed him to focus on the mile ahead had tumbled down.

He explained why he didn't like to have two-legged runners too close to him as he ran. "I'm running on one leg. It may not look like I'm running fast, but I'm going as hard as I can. It bothers me, people coming up beside me. I want to make those guys work. I can't stand making it easy for them. I'm really competitive. When they run with me, they're usually running for only two or three miles; for me it might be my twenty-sixth mile.

"Some people can't figure out what I'm doing. It's not a walk-hop, it's not a trot; it's running, or as close as I can get to running, and it's harder than doing it on two legs. It makes me mad when people call this a walk. If I was walking it wouldn't be anything.

"It's the difference between walking up a hill and walking up a mountain." The message was, of course, that Terry was on the mountain, not the hill.

Then the conversation turned to accomplishment. He said he spent a lot of his time thinking about life, about our carelessness on this planet. "Man is supposed to be an intelligent species, yet we keep polluting. We seem to want to wipe ourselves right off the earth, and no one is doing anything about it. That bothers me. Everyone seems to have given up hope of trying. I haven't. It isn't easy and it isn't supposed to be, but I'm accomplishing something. How many people give up a lot to do something good? I'm sure we would have found a cure for cancer twenty years ago if we had really tried.

"It bothers me, too, that so many kids are brought up the way they are. Why do we have crime? Why do we have so many thinking about themselves? You might think I'm a dreamer, but how many people would have said I could run across Canada? I know that there is $10 million out there to be given – if only everyone would try."

I asked Terry if he remembered any of his night dreams. He immediately said he didn't. It was clear he set store in the real world.

Then it was rest time. Terry and Doug disappeared with the van over a low hill to find a quiet, cool place to sleep for a few hours.

While they rested, Jack Hilliard, the Cancer Society's district representative who was responsible for Terry in eastern Ontario (and who also drove his car with the newly acquired and portable sign which said SLOW RUNNER AHEAD on one side and DONATIONS ACCEPTED HERE on the other), met with Jack Lambert, the district director who would take over in the Peterborough area. We drove through Rockland, while Darrell showed his fun-loving side and woke the sleepy town by calling on the loud-hailer: "Good morning, Rockland."

Already I found the routine tedious, and I had been with them less than twenty-four hours. Darrell claimed later that he was never bored.

"There wasn't a time when I said, 'What am I doing here?' because every day was different. You knew you'd meet someone new. Every day you were getting closer to home. I never wanted to go home, yet I dreamed of that day when he ran his last mile.

"You'd think I would be bored, getting up at 4:00 every day and sitting in that van, for how many hours. But it seemed that time went by fast. I never even got tired of getting his stuff ready or of making his sandwiches or giving him all that junk food."

By mid-afternoon, Terry was pushing himself hard along the main street of Rockland, quiet on this Sunday afternoon. Terry's OPP escort turned on his siren, and people streamed out of their houses or summer cottages. Those who were fit ran behind

Terry. The children on their bikes circled him like bees. Women ran up to Doug and asked if he would take their donations.

People stared hard at Terry, and from inside the van we watched their expressions change. You could see they were trying to understand what they were seeing. They looked amazed. Surely, they'd never seen anyone like Terry before. Then they clapped. They shouted after him. Some ran back into their houses to get someone else, so they, too, could see this remarkable runner.

It was like a parade. As I watched I talked to Doug. He had seen a lot of Canada from that viewpoint. "We eat, we go to bed, and we pass through these towns, and we don't get to see nothin'!" But he didn't seem to mind. It was just his realistic assessment of the job.

Then he turned and told me about Terry's heart condition. It was a deep secret, he said. Terry never talked about it. Despite the closeness and heat in the van, I felt a chill. Terry was taking more of a risk than any of us knew.

Doug wanted to be sure I understood that no matter how loud the cheers were, no matter how many people followed Terry and threw money into the van, despite all the attention and the circus-like atmosphere, Terry's journey was deadly serious. Terry had committed every part of his being, his entire life, to his cause.

Then Darrell rushed up, effervescent, euphoric, and broke the tension: "All right, all right!" he said as he listened to the applause. It was clear why he was on this journey, why he was never bored, why he never grew tired of his duties. He was in centre ring, serving his brother on the greatest adventure he would ever know. Everything he did was an act of love performed with grace and humour. His brother was running into the pages of Canadian history.

9

"I THINK YOU'VE ALL
HEARD MY STORY"

I f Darrell felt awkward wearing his shorts and T-shirt into Government House to meet Governor General Ed Schreyer and his wife, Lily, Terry certainly did not. He was brought a glass of orange juice on a silver tray, which he gulped down just as Schreyer came forward to meet him. Darrell remembered feeling stupid and uncomfortable when he accidentally dumped a glass of juice in the driveway of Government House. Besides, Darrell remembered, "there were all those guys from 'Reach for the Top,' wearing suits."

Ontario would be both exciting and taxing for Terry. He ran seven hundred miles out of his way, through the densely populated southern part of the province and the key fundraising cities of Toronto, Hamilton, and London. Doug shook his head in amazement. "Ontario was like eternity. We felt that we weren't going anywhere. Terry had conquered five provinces in two and a half months, and Ontario was equal to all of those. Two things I remember about Ontario: people everywhere, and money."

The groundswell of support that developed in Ontario eventually energized the entire country. There were small gestures and grand ones. For example, the children from the grade-five class in Odessa Public School (a village of four hundred, 165 miles east of Toronto) raised fifteen dollars by saving the pennies and nickels left over from their milk money. Their teacher, Brian Norris, promised to match whatever the children finally raised.

No less heartfelt was the effort made by two friends, Garth Walker of Mississauga and Jim Brown of Kingston, who found sponsors for their three-hundred-mile overnight dash from Toronto to Ottawa by bicycle. They raised more than $50,000 and cycled through thunderstorms to present the cash and pledges to Terry in person. But first he ran through Ottawa, where he encountered one of the warmest welcomes and the largest reception of his run to that point.

"When I ran through that tiny little Sparks Street Mall, the road was so narrow, yet people were running behind me and all these other people were lined up, clapping for me. It was quite a long way down the road where all the people were and I was just sprinting. I was floating through the air and I didn't even feel a thing. I felt so great. That type of memory you can never take away."

The next evening he had to choose to use either his good leg or his artificial leg for the kickoff of a Canadian Football League exhibition game between Ottawa and Saskatchewan. He chose his good leg.

He received a standing ovation from more than sixteen thousand fans at Lansdowne Park – he thought it was more exciting than watching Darryl Sittler score an overtime goal. He hadn't expected that kind of response from the crowd. He was beginning to understand that thousands upon thousands of ordinary Canadians were deeply moved by his effort. It made the struggle seem even more worthwhile.

He had run twenty miles that day and finished in time to drive back to Ottawa to meet Prime Minister Pierre Trudeau on Parliament Hill. Trudeau was just back from Venice and hadn't heard of the young runner. What should have been a highlight of Terry's trip was a disappointment.

They were scheduled to meet in Trudeau's Centre Block office, but as the prime minister walked up the stairs from the House of Commons, he was surprised to find Terry, his crew, and a gang of reporters waiting for him in the hallway. So they had the meeting there, against a background of stone walls and television lights.

Terry's hair was still damp with perspiration and clung to his forehead. He wore a T-shirt that said CANCER UNIT, GRAND FALLS, NEWFOUNDLAND on the back, his regulation grey, sweat-stained shorts and a dusty grey sock (which he hadn't changed since the start of the run) on his artificial leg. He was eager for Trudeau, an adventurer in his own right, to run a token half-mile with him. It would have had "a big effect on the campaign."

Trudeau, whose mind may have been on the grilling he'd received from the Opposition during Question Period, was as aloof as Terry was animated. His striped summer suit was crisp and he wore a fresh flower on his lapel.

Since there had been no time for a briefing by his press aides, Trudeau asked Terry basic questions: Which way was he running? Then he watched as Terry demonstrated how his artificial leg worked. Lights flashed down the stately hallway and the meeting was over. Darrell observed, "It was as if Trudeau was talking to Terry and thinking about something else." Terry wrote in his diary, "It was an honour to meet Mr. Trudeau who is a nice man. Unfortunately, he's very busy and can't run with me."

Terry said the meeting was not what he hoped it would be. "He didn't seem to know much about the run. I'm not blaming him – it was great meeting him – I just thought he knew more about it. He didn't even know I was running for cancer."

Two days later, on July 6, an editorial in the *Sunday Star* reflected the public's disappointment that Trudeau had failed to give Terry's run a boost: "This is a Prime Minister who has twirled a Yo-Yo on a state visit, pirouetted behind the Queen, slid down banisters, publicly somersaulted into swimming pools and canoed some of Canada's wildest rivers. For a man of such prowess, a half-mile run would scarcely make a dent in the prime ministerial schedule – and the cause is certainly deserving."

Terry's diary reflects the growing excitement as he ran through Ontario: "Unreal reception . . . tremendous support here . . . these people are really trying . . . best so far." He had been fitted for two new two-thousand-dollar legs, which would be made by a Hull prosthetist, one of Canada's most skilful craftsmen, Armand Viau. The War Amputations of Canada paid for the legs. At the same time, he was suffering more from large cysts that had formed on his stump. But Terry's ability to heal amazed even those who knew him well. Sometimes the sores would vanish overnight. Terry was also having difficulty sleeping, partly because of the heat, partly because of poorly sound-proofed hotel rooms and tension from the run.

People were now lining the highway to wait for him. They'd wait in the rain. Sometimes, when they hailed Doug's van to make a pledge, they'd explain that they had a sister who had also lost a leg to cancer. Sometimes they'd say nothing, just stand on the highway clapping when Terry ran by.

The drivers of Voyageur intercity buses got into the habit of stopping whenever they saw him. The driver would make an announcement on the loudspeaker, then walk to the back of the bus taking donations from passengers.

Sometimes the OPP escorts would find people were handing them money for the Marathon of Hope. "I can't take the money," one officer complained to Vigars after the first mile.

"By the second mile, he was driving with his hat out the window," Vigars said.

Some resented the duty until they met Terry. "They changed the moment they saw him run."

Once, near Millwood, Ontario, Terry collapsed in the van from exhaustion. His face was a brilliant red, his breath heavy, his eyes closed as if blocking out the light and the pain. He had a wrinkled hundred-dollar bill clasped in his hand. He was oblivious to everything – visitors, well-wishers, even the money. He needed a rest. Jack Lambert made arrangements for Terry to take his break at the home of Olga Fallis, a Cancer Society volunteer. When Terry walked into her ninety-seven-year-old brick farmhouse, he was asked how long he'd like to sleep. He smiled wanly and said, "Till I wake up!"

Doug followed him, bringing fresh clothes and a can of spaghetti to be warmed for Terry's lunch.

In the next few days, Doug noticed a change. Terry wasn't greeted merely as the one-legged runner; he was greeted as a celebrity, a folk hero, a Canadian wonder. He was filmed by NBC's "Real People" and ran with hostess-interviewer Sarah Purcell. A picture of them together appeared on the front page of the *Toronto Sun*.

When Terry walked into an Oshawa shopping mall, Doug recalled, "It was as if he was a rock star. People were crowding around wanting to touch him. It was packed from one end to the other, and I couldn't even see him when he started to leave. Women and girls, teenagers especially, were starting to chase him. I'm sure he started to wonder, 'What's happening?'"

The next morning, the *Toronto Star* arranged to have Rolly, Betty, and Judith delivered by a long blue limousine to a quiet street corner in Whitby, just before dawn, for a surprise reunion with Terry as he came over a hill. The air was fine, and women stood on the sidewalk, wearing sweaters over their nighties, waiting for Terry to run into sight. The family embraced in front of the cameras.

Then Terry refused to pose any more and rested for a few minutes in a doughnut shop. While Terry attacked the can of beans brought from the van, his parents looked at him carefully and liked what they saw. He looked healthier and stronger than he had in Nova Scotia. They longed to be alone with him. As Rolly said, "It's hard to talk to your son in public," but Terry, in those days, could have had anything he wanted except privacy.

As Betty and Rolly watched him, Terry chatted amiably about how nice it was to see his parents, adding he felt they were always with him anyway. From the doughnut shop, a radio broadcaster could be heard telling listeners about Terry Fox and how they could see him running on Highway 2 later that day. Terry refused to get in the limousine that would take him and his parents to a hotel to rest: he said it was pretentious.

Terry's schedule was unpredictable, but people were willing to wait hours for his arrival and be content to give him a shout when he finally passed by. John and Edna Neale, a retired Pickering couple, waited two hours on a hot day. As Terry ran by, they said he was just what was needed to give Canadians a little pride, the same kind of pride Americans have in abundance.

A pair of thirteen-year-old girls, Linda Rowe and Patricia Morrison, were anxious to get Terry's autograph. But those days were over, too. He didn't have time, Doug explained, as he returned the girls' crumpled scraps of paper. "We want to remember him when we get older," Linda said.

On the outskirts of Metropolitan Toronto, Molly and Fred Danniels sat in garden chairs on their front lawn. They sipped coffee, ate cheesecake, and waited. Molly wanted to do something for Terry, so she painted a sign at least four feet square that said GOOD LUCK, TERRY. Terry didn't run by their house all day, so the Dannielses got up at 5:00 to catch him the next morning.

Terry seemed to appeal to everyone. A cab driver woke his children up at 4:30 and drove to Kingston Road in Scarborough so they would see Terry and never forget. He passed twenty-five dollars to Doug and said, "It's from me and the kids." A scary-looking motorcyclist, shrouded in black leather, pulled up beside the van in the early-morning dark, thrust a twenty-dollar bill through the open window, and drove away without a word.

In Scarborough, Terry made his most moving speech. He seemed to need to speak in public about what was bothering him in private. The weight of the Marathon of Hope was heavy on him these days. Just as he had once confessed he was some-times hard on Doug, he now stood beneath a swirl of curved bal-conies, crowded with adoring fans, in the airy cavern of the Scarborough Civic Centre, and told several thousand people that being famous wasn't important to him. "I'm overwhelmed. This is unreal," he began. "I think you've all heard my story . . ." He paused as the crowd applauded. "One thing hurts me. I keep hearing 'Terry Fox.'

"I'm not doing the run to become rich or famous. One of the problems with our world is that people are getting greedy and selfish." He wasn't receiving a cent of the money he raised, he said.

"To me, being famous is not the idea of the run. The only important part is that cancer can be beaten." Don't forget that, he told them, and focus your thoughts on the Marathon of Hope, not on him. There were people behind the scenes – he mentioned Darrell and Doug, even his police escort – who were working hard, he said. If you have any complaints about the Marathon of Hope, don't blame other people, blame him, he said. He was no better, no different than anyone else. He was wiping his eyes as he spoke.

"Even if I don't finish, we need others to continue. It's got to keep going without me," he said.

Doug shook his head in amazement as he listened to Terry. "I can't believe the kind of person he's become since grade eight."

But Darrell saw it differently: "To me he hasn't changed. He's been so close to death – he has such a good feeling for life."

Terry was tearful, his voice husky and strained. In his hand he held a daffodil, which had been given to him by Anne Marie Von Zuben, a victim of kidney cancer since age three, who looked much younger than her thirteen years. The sight of Anne Marie, whose mother called her a miracle baby because of her many recoveries, whose smile and positive attitude seemed the essence of the Marathon of Hope, was almost too much for Terry. For a man who was reticent, who was sometimes difficult to interview because he was saying the same things repeatedly, this was a rare moment of revelation. It didn't come after hours of intense questioning; it came in front of a crowd of ordinary people. He was speaking spontaneously about what was on his mind. It was a heartbreaking moment.

He remembered that moment, too. "Everyone sounded close and warm. Just looking at people, way up on the top row, curled all the way around, cheering and clapping, I felt really close to them, warm and emotional, and I think they felt the same way, too. The biggest thing was when the little girl brought up the flower. She's the one who really broke me down. The way the room was built, I could really feel the vibrations coming back to me. It wasn't planned. It's just the way I felt at the time. That moment, right then, was one of the highest."

Vigars said they had very nearly cancelled Terry's visit to the Scarborough Civic Centre, because Terry was worried he wasn't spending enough time with his parents on their brief visit. Nothing had prepared them for a reception on such a large scale, with such emotional impact. "From then on, it became almost uncontrollable, and we had to just go with the flow as much as possible," Vigars said.

The plan for Toronto was complicated. After Scarborough, Terry was going to run from Bloor Street down University Avenue to an important rally in Nathan Phillips Square. He'd take a plane the next morning, a Saturday, for a side trip to Niagara Falls. That afternoon, back in Toronto, he'd make his way into the heart of downtown, running along Danforth Avenue.

Sunday morning, he'd set out from Nathan Phillips Square to Lakeshore Boulevard and head west towards Oakville and the cities of southern Ontario. But first, there was a surprise meeting with his brother Fred, also flown in by the *Toronto Star*, and the long-awaited introduction to Toronto Maple Leafs team captain, Darryl Sittler.

It was a bright, hot summer day, and the temperature reached thirty degrees Celsius. With Doug, Darrell, Fred, Judith, and Darryl Sittler beside him, Terry ran down Toronto's University Avenue through lunch-hour traffic. They passed the University of Toronto, on one side, Queen's Park, the Ontario legislature, on the other, on down the broad boulevard past Canada's teaching and research hospitals. Women in hair curlers peered out of chic beauty salons and called their stylists over to have a look as Terry ran by. Others hiked up their summer skirts and ran on high heels to get a second look at him. Medical technicians, their white lab coats flapping, ran down the street beside him, and volunteers wove in and out of traffic to fill garbage bags with donations.

In photographs of the two of them running, Sittler is seen smiling easily while Terry's face is contorted into that familiar grimace. It was clear there was a great difference between running on two good legs and running on one made of fibre-glass and steel.

The group entered Nathan Phillips Square, where about ten thousand waited, and went to a stage where politicians, company executives, entertainers, and Cancer Society officers led by actor Al Waxman, the society's honorary chairman, waited. Sittler gave Terry his 1980 NHL all-star team sweater, number 27, and called Terry a superstar: "I've been around athletes a long time and I've never seen any with his courage and stamina." The gift meant a great deal to both Sittler and Terry, who put it on immediately.

Betty, Rolly, Fred, and Judith were led onstage, and as Rolly approached Terry, he spontaneously lifted his son's hand in victory. Terry quickly drew his hand back down. Then Waxman introduced Terry as the "toast of Toronto and the hero of all Canada."

Terry faced the crowd, on whose faces tears mingled with beads of perspiration, and told them a little of the problems of heroism. "It almost hurts me to walk down a road and have people grab my hand and ask for my autograph and not sit and talk. When I'm finished I'm not going to be on the front page, but I'm going to be just as happy without the publicity. . . .

"Those claps, take them for yourself. If you've given a dollar, you are part of the Marathon of Hope. That ovation was for you, wherever you are in Canada."

The Cancer Society estimated about $100,000 was gathered in one day. Of that sum, $59,000 came in pledges through broadcaster Jeremy Brown's efforts on CKFM radio, which reported listeners phoned in pledges at a rate of four thousand dollars per hour. That night, Terry threw the opening pitch of a Toronto Blue Jays baseball game and received a standing ovation at Exhibition Stadium.

The next morning, he flew to Niagara Falls and was handed a cheque for one hundred dollars by the mayor, Wayne Thompson, and was greeted by fifty people. It was an embarrassment to the city, fumed Cliff Gregory, president of the Cancer Society, because the town offered Terry neither moral nor monetary support. Terry refused to visit a Niagara Falls Marineland show when he was told he wouldn't be able to raise funds. Nothing could make him angrier than the thought that he was being used commercially. He'd go out of his way to speak to people, but he had to be sure he could raise money on those visits.

Later that day, Terry was back in Toronto, and I caught him for a few minutes before he started his afternoon run along Danforth Avenue, the city's traffic-choked Greek strip. We had a hasty interview:

"What do you think of the attention?"

"It's great that they like me, but they should give a buck, too," he said.

A few more questions, and I said, "Thanks, Terry. Good luck on your walk."

I felt like a clod as his eyes turned steely and he said, "I'm running."

It was a muggy, overcast, very hot day. Volunteers were recruited off the street to collect donations from drivers stalled behind Terry and the Metro Toronto motorcycle police who preceded him. A dark-haired young man asked his girlfriend to take over the wheel of his red Corvette, while he ran eight miles into town helping to collect money. He refused to give his name. A photographer turned his back on a wedding party to photograph Terry.

"Top fellow!" called a British voice from a passing car.

"Magnificent, man!" yelled someone else.

The loudest shouts came from people who stood outside bars to watch Terry pass.

Later, Terry's family and a couple of Cancer Society volunteers emptied the garbage bags filled with money onto the creamy carpet at the Four Seasons Hotel. Betty hadn't watched

Terry run; she found it too painful. Terry sat back beaming with a bottle of beer. They counted $5,326.26, collected in about two hours of running. Included in one of those bags was a letter from a Toronto woman who wrote that Terry had helped her stop feeling sorry for herself. She vowed to lose weight and she pledged Terry one dollar for every pound lost. Her husband, she added, would match her dollar for dollar. The last line read: "P.S. This could mean $200."

When the last pile of pennies was tucked away in a drawer, Doug puffed in, looking more confused than usual. "Where'd everyone go?" he asked. He was so excited, he had run along Bloor Street for an extra mile, long after Terry had turned in at the hotel. Doug probably would have kept running, enjoying the exercise and his joyful release from the driver's seat, if a puzzled Metro police constable hadn't asked him where he was going and pointed him back to the hotel.

Isadore Sharp spent some time with Terry and suggested he think about the future. "This is just the beginning of what you can do, and you should be thinking of it before you get to Vancouver. Let's talk about it," Sharp had said. Later Sharp, remembering that conversation, said, "I think he knew, that he was slowly feeling his body weaken. He wouldn't talk about the future."

That night the family relaxed together over a meal in the world's highest restaurant, which was just below the world's highest disco, atop the CN Tower. The lights on the tower's top, which usually read SPARKLES, said TERRY FOX that night. Terry started to doze over his half-finished dinner, but he revived later in the tower's basement penny arcade.

It was a rare evening. For once he had a chance to unwind. All the Fox offspring jumped into bumper cars and rammed one another hard, and laughed even harder. Terry's leg was jogged loose, and he had to limp, holding his artificial limb, which was hidden under corduroy pants, off the platform. Suddenly he was surrounded by autograph-seekers.

"Nobody recognized me until my leg fell off," he laughed.

Hamilton, Brantford, London, Kitchener, Guelph, and Brampton – all the southern Ontario cities welcomed Terry. The response to his fundraising drive was unexpected. For example, Joan Gibb, an Oakville Cancer Society volunteer, reported that a week before Terry arrived, about $235 had been collected. She decided to have an oversized cheque made up for the presentation. But when Darrell arrived to help with advance work around 4:00 p.m. she had to alter the total to $8,600. When Terry arrived two hours later, the figure had jumped to $11,239.

Crowds were as constant and in some ways as debilitating as the high temperatures. Everyone wanted to be close to Terry. They wanted him to make speeches, to accept cheques, and to do so in person.

In Hamilton, it was reported, Terry was mobbed by teenagers and women after he spoke at the Royal Botanical Gardens. He raised $4,500 there. A story sent by the wire service described Terry as "irritable" and needing a nap. It was also in Hamilton, however, that 1960 Canadian Marathon champion Gord Dickson gave Terry his gold medal, saying the young fellow was running the greatest race of all.

While he would never accept money for himself (although it was common for someone to press fifty dollars into his hand and say, "Keep it. This is for you. For yourself.") Terry accepted mementos. All cash gifts went to the Cancer Society.

In mid-July, a curious item appeared in the *Guelph Daily Mercury*. A seventeen-year-old high-school student, Marlene Lott, was quoted saying there was "nothing extra-curricular" about her relationship with Terry, despite a *Toronto Sun* photograph showing her kneeling in the van, wiping Terry's neck with a towel. She said she had developed a "slight friendship" with Terry's sister, Judith, during her five-day stay in Toronto. Marlene and Terry went for dinner a few times, but nothing was more important to Terry than the run. Nothing could distract him from his goal. The fact remained, however, that Terry was an attractive and now famous young man who was sometimes lonely, though people were always around him.

Terry realized that he had to be above reproach. He had become a celebrity and events around him were becoming complicated. He was being watched and he was being reported on. Once the *Star* reported he had gone on a date. He felt that information was personal, not something to be reported in a newspaper. So, rather than subject himself, or anyone else, to the media's probing eye, he simply said to himself, no girls.

"You know, I hardly ever had the chance to meet anybody. I was just too busy, and when I did, it was publicized. But my goal was so strong overall that it didn't really bother me. It didn't really affect me, but there were some times when I wished that I could meet somebody, or I'd see a girl and be attracted back and want to ask her out. I guess that just makes me more human. But it never was a big sacrifice. I knew my goal. I could wait."

Occasionally, Terry needed someone to talk to about matters that were troubling him. He called me at home one Saturday afternoon. First, he said he was sorry he hadn't been able to talk to me for the previous "Running with Terry" report. Then, warming to his subject, he complained that he couldn't make a move without someone reporting on it. Lastly, he asked how I thought the public would react if a girl joined the Marathon of Hope for a couple of weeks. "You know me," Terry said. "I have high morals." After some discussion we both agreed that in conservative southern Ontario, a girl on her own would

only invite unwanted curiosity and speculation. He didn't really
need convincing. I suspect he knew it all along. He just needed
to talk about being lonely.

The days that followed were difficult for Terry. Temperatures
soared to thirty-eight degrees Celsius and a muggy wind slowed
his progress, yet he continued to run twenty-six miles a day, or
very close to it. In London he was escorted by a hundred runners
who had each raised fifty dollars in pledges. They called themselves the $5,000 Club, but might as well have been called the
$11,000 Club – because that's how much they raised. Terry also
ran with seventeen-year-old Tony Coutinho, a leukemia survivor
for twelve and a half years and the subject of the Emmy-winning
documentary *Fighting Back*.

In Stratford, Terry got a kiss from British actress and festival star Maggie Smith between fittings for a new leg by his
British Columbia prosthetist, Ben Speicher, who had been flown
to London courtesy of the War Amputations of Canada. His
stump was in surprisingly good condition, according to prosthetists who had examined him along the way.

Terry was elated to see him. "I started out on a leg he built
and I'm back using it again," he told reporters. "I had two new
legs made in [Hull] Quebec, but they haven't stood up. I'll feel a
lot better when I have the spare leg made. I've been worried
about the leg breaking down and losing a lot of time waiting."

As he ran through the southern Ontario heat, which clung
to him and sapped his strength, and made him feel as if he were
running in slow motion, Terry heard radio reports that he was
sick and in bad shape.

"Don't believe everything you hear," he warned a Vancouver
interviewer. "One of the radio stations out here said I would be
in the hospital for three days. No way."

The run also had its funny moments. Darrell often sat on
the hood of a donations car as it crawled along the highway,

accepting money from drivers as they passed. Once a driver pulled up to Darrell, not understanding what was going on. He looked in the hat, saw all the money, and took out five dollars. Darrell looked at him in amazement and said thank you as the driver pulled away and disappeared down the road.

Some of the fundraising gimmicks were laughable, too. Freddie Sless of Hamilton raised $912 for Terry by sitting in a huge vat of banana-lemon custard. "I didn't notice the smell at first," he told reporters, "but then I was starting to get hazy." Brad Barber of Mississauga put on a pair of kneepads and vowed to break a world record for crawling, in Terry's honour. He made eleven and a half miles, short of the fourteen-mile record, before giving up. He raised five thousand dollars.

The marathon machine was in high gear. Money was rolling in to the Cancer Society at such a rapid rate, they couldn't count it efficiently. By July 21, the society reported it had received $750,000 in cash but couldn't estimate the amount of pledges. Ron Calhoun guessed that they'd collected $20,000 in one day in southern Ontario.

Jon Hurst was on holiday at his Lake Simcoe cottage. He got up at 4:00 a.m., filled the car with friends and family, and drove to a spot on Highway 11 to wait for Terry. They stood in the dark and Hurst noticed others had the same idea. Soon about forty people were gathered around them. Despite the crowd, there was silence as everyone stared down the highway. Finally, they saw in the distance the red flash of the OPP cruiser. Before they saw Terry's outline in the light of the cruiser's headlamps, they could hear the *thump, thump* of his footfall on the highway.

Hurst was preparing to say something meaningful to Terry as he ran by. But he watched in silence, unable to utter a word.

Later, Hurst remembered Bill Vigars selling Terry Fox T-shirts out of the back of his car. Hurst looked in the trunk, saw boxes of T-shirts, boxes filled with money, and piles of dirty laundry. Such was life on the road.

Terry appeared worn out, but his recuperative ability was immense. One night's good sleep could cure a week of stress, but he was rarely allowed even that. Terry told a reporter, "People want me everywhere. The Cancer Society people have been really great, but they don't understand that I get tired at night."

Once organizers even expected him to be in two places at the same time. Forgetting that Terry had promised, months before, to attend a lunch in Toronto with 140 senior executives, the Cancer Society scheduled him to speak in Brampton at the same time. It was awkward. Some thought, wrongly, that Terry preferred to spend an afternoon with Canada's corporate elite, instead of the working people of Brampton. The *Brampton Daily Times* even accused the Cancer Society of using Terry to further its fundraising ambitions. (Terry's answer to those claims was that the Cancer Society wasn't using him enough.) If only the people of Brampton could have seen how unimpressed Terry was by the hotel silver-plate, the chilled strawberries, and the fresh-cut flowers at the lunch.

Canada's corporate leaders were shaking Terry's hand and patting him on the back. There they were, in their finely tailored three-piece suits, and there was Terry, in his T-shirt and shorts. He was calm and confident as ever, and apparently interested in everyone he met. The then mayor of Toronto came over to Terry and said, "I'm John Sewell. I'm the mayor." Pauline McGibbon, the province's lieutenant-governor at the time, was chatting with Terry, her husband, Don, by her side.

The party was thrown by Isadore Sharp, who initiated the corporate challenge and presented Terry with a cheque for $10,600 – honouring in advance his pledge of two dollars every mile Terry would run across Canada. Sharp hoped the other CEOs would respond with similar donations.

Terry believed his speech to the executives was one of his best and wrote in his diary that he felt he made a good impression. In fact, he charmed them inside out. He told them about cancer research and about the drug that had improved his odds for survival from 15 per cent to between 50 and 70 per cent. He told them it was more difficult losing his hair than losing his leg, but "that turned out good because I never had curly hair before and now I do." They heard him chuckle as he laughed at his own vanity, and they watched his face tense as he described his young friend from the cancer clinic who kept him awake with his screams of pain.

He was by now a practised and artful public speaker. He told them that, although it sounded crass, money, their money, was needed to fight cancer. Then he told them how other Canadians were responding. A man had given Terry his five-hundred-dollar guitar with tears in his eyes. Young kids had given him ten cents – everything they had. Pensioners and welfare recipients were giving more than they could probably afford. "It's important to give what you can, to give money, because you want to find a cure. It feels good to give."

He told them people could get cancer and die from it and still be winners. He told them he would never be called a quitter. Then he repeated a couple of sentences that made a few in his audience feel uneasy. Not that it was prophetic, not that Terry had second sight, or even a premonition of what was to come. It was just that he seemed so healthy. He beamed and sparkled with strength and good humour. "If I stop," he said, "it's because something's happened. I'm in bed but I'm still going to think of myself as a winner."

He knew just how good it felt to give.

Later, Terry knocked knees with Bobby Orr, the former hockey star and the Canadian Terry had most wanted to meet, who presented him with a cheque for $25,000 from his sponsors,

Planter's Peanuts. It was, Terry told his diary, the highlight of his trip.

The next days had both highs and lows. Terry wanted to run, only run. Yet he found himself driving the van thirty miles at night to receptions, and that drained him. He found that Bill Vigars and Bill O'Connor, another district director, had arranged for him to run an extra ten miles out of his way to Barrie, along Highway 11, instead of Highway 27, and speak at two receptions. He was furious, yet powerless.

Vigars had agreed to the longer route without consulting Terry, believing Terry would be pleased with the extra fundraising opportunity. Terry insisted he would take the shorter route. Vigars, bringing Terry's clubhouse sandwich and French fries to his hotel room, begged him to reconsider. He said the Cancer Society was worried that volunteers in the area might quit if Terry didn't come and that he might even be fired. Terry threw the sandwich in Vigars's direction and stormed out.

Terry, silent with rage, hurt because he no longer had control over his own run, and close to exhaustion, ran the ten miles up Highway 11. He spoke at the two receptions, but he didn't speak to Vigars for three days.

The two had become close friends by this time. Vigars, struggling with a marriage breakdown, was on the road with Terry for two and a half months, often with his children. Sometimes Terry played with the children at night, because they were distraction from the tensions of the day.

"Bill let other Cancer Society people know that only one thing was supposed to be planned for me at night and he'd tell them what time I'd arrive. If I didn't make it to a town I would drive to it. He was there for all those special things. But he was more than that because he became a close friend. I think he was a real good guy, friendly, joking all the time. I could relax with him. He was somebody who began to care a lot about me. I could talk to him about anything I wanted and ask advice. Before he came, I really didn't have anything like that. There are things that I can talk to Doug about, and he's great, but there are some things I can't – I don't know why. And Darrell, well, he was my younger brother.

"If something was bugging me, if there was a girl or somebody who wanted to get involved with the trip and I didn't know how to say she or he couldn't, Bill would do it for me. He would do the dirty work. At the same time, sometimes things got boggled up because he wasn't quite sure. He made some mistakes, too, but I don't hold anything against him. Just as I got upset at Darrell and Doug, sometimes I got upset with Bill. He's not the type of person who could take it, and sometimes he would leave for a few days just because of that, and then come back. On our way to Sault Ste. Marie, he left for three days. I was upset, because Doug and Darrell never left. They were always there. Bill was supposed to be travelling with us all the way but he needed a rest inside to keep going. It bothered me. I thought it was a weakness that the rest of us didn't have."

Vigars saw himself as mother and father to the whole crew. He was sometimes caught in the middle between the Cancer Society's expectations and Terry's. Society officials were saying he was spending too much time on the run, and sometimes he would leave to make arrangements for Terry farther down the road.

His patience was waning, too. Near Barrie, Vigars thought Terry was getting a little cocky, even rude, and was annoyed when he heard a tone in Terry he'd never heard before. An official came up to Terry, put out his hand, gave his name, and said, "I'm the reeve." Bill was shocked to hear Terry reply, "Big deal."

On another occasion, Bill heard a passerby looking at the mileage indicator, a chart on the side of the van that showed how far Terry had run and had yet to run, which showed Terry was two hundred miles short of halfway: "Congratulations on being halfway."

Terry: "Can't you add?"

Terry, however, didn't remember the incident. Perhaps the demands were too much for him. Perhaps that's the only way Terry could react. Whenever he took a break somebody wanted his autograph, somebody wanted to talk to him or touch him. On the road there were no buffers. He was exposed.

In the evenings, when the receptions were over and the miles were marked off for the night, Terry had a different personality. He was lighthearted, not intense and demanding. He was the jokester everyone remembered. There may have been undercurrents of tension, but their foundation was love and deep respect. Doug, Darrell, and Bill were understanding and forgiving. They knew that Terry was right: they were bungling at his expense.

Darrell remembered once trying to alter the mileage indicator. Darrell changed the miles but he had the numbers wrong. Terry yelled at him to get it right. Darrell changed it again, but he was wrong a second time. Terry took him aside and patiently explained all Darrell had to do was add four.

"And I was trying so hard to get it right!" Darrell said.

As they approached Gravenhurst and Terry's twenty-second birthday, his friends plotted how they could surprise him. Darrell was assigned to walk towards Terry and throw a whipped-cream cake at him. But then there was a change in plan. Terry might not take a pie in the face very well; better just to hand it to him.

Terry ran twelve miles through the rain, past crowds of people who sang "Happy Birthday" at every corner. It was comical and touching. Some bystanders wore plastic garbage bags to repel the rain; others protected their heads with paper bags.

As Terry walked into the Holiday Inn, Darrell made his respectful approach, cake in hand. Terry received it gently, then hurled it towards Darrell. He fired remaining bits towards Scott Hamilton filming the events, and towards Vigars. They were all laughing, and covered in cake, as they walked into the Holiday Inn for breakfast – Black Forest cake and Coke. Terry's sole birthday wish had been to run twenty-six miles; he wouldn't consider taking a day, or even a half-day, off. Because of all the festivities, he only had time for twenty miles that day – but what a day!

He was invited for dinner at the Beaver Creek Correctional Camp, a minimum-security federal penitentiary where the inmates had raised nine hundred dollars in a car wash and a barbecue for his marathon. One of the men stood spontaneously to tell Terry, "I've been through some of the toughest jails in Canada and been with some of the hardest men, but you have more guts and courage than any I ever met."

Compliments also came from the other side of the law. Ontario Provincial Police Constable John Lennox of the Bala detachment was Terry's escort through cottage country. He called his assignment the proudest days of his life. "If all kids had his honesty, guts, and desire, I'd be out of a job."

Terry was rushed back to the Gravenhurst Civic Centre, where two thousand people gathered to sing "Happy Birthday." Terry's gifts included his new limb from Ben Speicher, a toilet seat inscribed "To a good shit," and a *Playboy* magazine. The latter two were Bill's ideas. Telegrams poured in from across Canada, including a long one from the British Columbia Cancer Society, which bore a thousand signatures and a donation of $4,000.

The biggest thrill of all – which made Terry's face radiate happiness – was the news that Gravenhurst, a town of eight thousand, raised $14,000. It was close to double Terry's dream of one dollar from every Canadian. Everyone shared a seventy-pound cake decorated with a map of Canada that showed Terry's route in red and green icing, and marked Gravenhurst with a red cherry. It was donated by Peter Rebelein of the Gravenhurst Bakery. The next day, Terry's photograph was on the front page of the *Vancouver Sun*, his head peeking through the toilet seat. The Cancer Society was not happy with Vigars for allowing Terry to pose in such an undignified fashion.

Terry wore his new leg the next morning, and after nine miles his stump was raw and bloodied. He broke for a rest and a shower and the water scalded his stump, but he put on his old leg and did another eleven miles. A local reporter spotted the blood and the wire service was alerted.

Reporters got on the telephone to the War Amps in Ottawa and asked what Terry's chances were of making it. Cliff Chadderton, the association's chief executive, predicted Terry was going to run into "terrible problems" because of the beating inflicted upon the stump.

Terry didn't think anyone had seen the blood. He was used to it. However, he was not used to having alarm bells go off every time he bled. Where was all the concern when he and Doug were alone on the highway in Newfoundland and blood was pouring out of his knee joint? He was angry and belligerent, especially when asked if he would see a doctor.

"I'd see a doctor if I had to, but that depends on what you mean by 'had to,'" he said. "There's no doctor in the world who's had an amputee who's doing anything on an artificial limb like I am. If I went to see a doctor he'd have a pessimistic approach. What if he did tell me it was okay to keep going and then a week later something happened? Then he'd be in trouble and have to defend himself.

"I appreciate their concern for me. I don't care what a doctor tells me. I'm going to keep running." Chadderton said he was disturbed by the reports he was getting from Ontario prosthetists who had examined Terry's stump in Toronto, Hamilton, and London. Terry argued that all of those specialists had told him that his stump was in good condition.

The War Amputations of Canada predicted Terry would soon not be able to tolerate the pain and suggested he should take a break and consult a specialist. They were in a delicate position. Said Chadderton, "The guy is so tremendous, but if anyone utters one word of criticism, it looks like we're not supporting him. We are worried because the prosthetic reports are coming back to us saying the stump is changing shape, it's developing sores and is not in good condition. He should be seeing an orthopedic man to check for proper blood flow. The run is very positive and we'd hate to see it abandoned because he's had no medical attention."

But the last word was Terry's. He insisted he knew his own body better than anyone else: "Maybe that's why I've made it as far as I have – 2,521 miles. If I ran to a doctor every time I got a little cyst or abrasion I'd still be in Nova Scotia. Or else I'd never have started. I've seen people in so much pain. The little bit of pain I'm going through is nothing. They can't shut it off, and I can't shut down every time I feel a little sore."

Terry said this on the shore of Lake St. Joseph, near Foot's Bay. To the untrained eye, the tender stump, the cause of the uproar, seemed to have been only slightly skinned.

He ran twenty-six miles that day and his parting shot was "Not bad for a guy who's supposed to be heading for the hospital."

10

"TODAY WAS A DIFFICULT DAY"

The bleeding-stump episode marked another change for the participants in the Marathon of Hope. Once, shortly afterwards, Doug remembered, Terry, hurting and proud, climbed into the van and said, "Get out. I want to cry alone." Something was different.

Doug was puzzled. Was the stump bothering Terry more than he would say? Darrell, who was perhaps more intuitive, sensed that something was wrong. He watched Terry as he ran, and felt each step took too much effort. He seemed to have lost the ease and comfort that had marked his stride in New Brunswick and Quebec. Darrell knew Terry had a bad temper, but felt this new attitude was different. He knew his brother was self-willed and stubborn, but he was not irritable by nature.

Darrell kept looking for reasons to explain the change. Was it the heat? Was it the hills of northern Ontario? Was it the lack of sleep? Day after day, Terry recorded in his diary that he was waking up exhausted. Doug and Darrell withdrew from Terry just a step. They would be there when he called them, but it seemed that those days he needed to be alone.

Terry had by now left the crowds behind. His path along Highway 69 took him along the wild eastern shore of Georgian Bay.

There were good times, too; there always were with Terry. In Parry Sound he met Bobby Orr's father, Doug, who presented Terry with "the greatest gift I've ever been given," Bobby's Canada Cup sweater and a large photo of the hockey legend flying through the air after scoring an overtime goal to win the 1970 Stanley Cup. Terry felt he was in heaven.

Jack Lambert, the paternal Cancer Society district director who accompanied Terry through central Ontario, left the run south of Sudbury. With his round belly and Bermuda shorts, Lambert had become a familiar figure on the highway. He had driven hundreds of miles behind Terry at a speed of one or two miles an hour, his right hand on the wheel, his left hand stretched out the window to receive donations from passersby. His job had been to arrange for local receptions, to make sure volunteers were stirring up enthusiasm, and, most of all, to make sure that Terry was happy.

Doug saw Lambert as "a man with a heart who backed Terry all the way." Terry responded to that loyalty, and the day Lambert left was a sad one. "I'll miss him," Terry told his diary. "He was great!"

On August 4 Terry learned that the van's odometer had been measuring his miles incorrectly and that he had already passed the halfway mark. The 4-per-cent error in the odometer reading allowed them to add an extra sixty-five miles to his total. But Terry refused to regard the blunder as a boon. His pattern of goal-setting – he had been running towards the halfway mark for days – was upset. The psychological spark he would receive by crossing the midpoint had been snatched away from him. Terry fell into a funk for a few days, but rallied.

August 7, near Blind River
2,734 miles

> Today was a great day. I finished twenty-six miles by 3:20 p.m. First I did fourteen miles then I did twelve. The morning was very cool. In fact, I had to wear a sweater for the first two miles. The miles were strong and solid until the final mile of the day, when I nearly collapsed. Got that empty, weak feeling when the heat and humidity get to me.

Terry was congratulated on passing the halfway mark for the next four hundred miles. It was already a sore point. His fans on the roadside couldn't have known they were testing his patience with their friendly little signs. Terry said later, "The halfway point really bothered me. I hit halfway just before Sudbury. I get to Sault Ste. Marie and I figure it's all downhill, mileage-wise. I've run more miles than I'll have to for the rest of the trip. I knew what I had done and how it affected me psychologically. Then I see this huge sign: COME ON, TERRY, YOU'RE HALFWAY. LET'S GO ALL THE WAY. Maybe they didn't know what I'd done. Thunder Bay and Sault Ste. Marie have competitions all the time and always argue over who's halfway. Maybe that's why they put the sign up. The first thing I said when I saw that sign was 'I'm more than halfway.' I couldn't wait to get past that sign. In Wawa, maybe Marathon and Nipigon, the official halfway mark, I heard it a lot. There were tiny signs everywhere and I'd stop and actually explain to the people that I'd passed halfway. It was important."

By August 12, Terry had raised $1.4 million and Canadians across the country knew his story. Dorothy Stone of Georgetown,

Ontario, started a campaign to nominate him for the Order of Canada. She urged Canadians to flood the office of the Secretariat of Honours with the name Terry Fox. Steve Milton, then a sports columnist for the *Orillia Packet and Times*, recommended he be named the Canadian Press athlete of the year. The Cancer Society was still boggled by his impact and could scarcely handle the five hundred pledges and donations that daily flooded the Ontario division office.

Terry was also eliciting some concerned comment. "GIVE IT UP, TERRY," read a headline over a *Peterborough Examiner* editorial. "It's not a celebration of life to push heroic gesture to the point of self damage. . . . If he now deliberately incurs new suffering a thousand hearts made stronger by his example will falter at his folly." Crusty broadcaster Gordon Sinclair called Terry a three-legged horse who should be stopped. And from the Sault *Daily Star*: "Terry Fox has done a magnificent job of rousing the concern of Canadians for others. Now concerned Canadians should implore him to call off his effort before he jeopardizes his entire future."

The worst, by Terry's reckoning, came from the *Globe and Mail*, in which he was painted as a tyrannical brother while Darrell had the Cinderella role of van-sweeper. The report said he was running because he held a grudge against a doctor who had misdiagnosed his condition at Simon Fraser. "Trash," Terry grumbled. The clincher was the *Globe*'s quote of the day. The luckless Lou Fine, Jack Lambert's successor, was reported as saying, "It was the society that made the success. He's only doing the running."

Unlike others who read that quote, Terry was not bothered by it. He reasoned that indeed he was only doing the running, and that perhaps he hadn't given the society or its volunteers the credit they deserved. But he was upset when he heard that Fine's job was in jeopardy because of his indiscretion. Terry announced that if Fine lost his job, he would stop running for the Cancer Society. While the phone jangled at the society offices for a few days, the overall impact of Fine's indiscretion was positive: donations to the Marathon of Hope poured in faster than ever.

What hurt Terry most of all was that he didn't know whom in the media to trust. He saw the Marathon of Hope as a positive force. If reporters were going to write negatively about his efforts, he decided he wouldn't have anything more to do with them. "They missed the point completely," he said. "If they are not positive about the run, I won't talk to them. I'm not here to play games with the media. I don't need all that extra pressure."

The state of his temper was, he felt, not front-page news. Although it was true, as reported, that Darrell had said that Terry sometimes took his frustrations out on him, Terry was annoyed by what the reporter had left out: "He didn't write down the fact that Darrell, at the exact time, also said, 'I don't mind because I know what he's going through. I know what he goes through every day. He's running all day long. I can take it if I have to. If that's going to help him, if it'll help relieve his frustrations, I don't mind.'

"We had good times, too. We went out to dinner and Doug and Darrell and I used to joke and fool around a lot. There were days when I felt good and nobody wrote about that. And it wasn't always me. Darrell and Doug had a fist fight. I don't know if anybody else knows about it. They had a fight about a radio station. Darrell wanted it on and Doug wanted it off, so Doug punched Darrell and Darrell punched him back and gave him a bleeding nose." Twenty minutes later, Darrell added, they were all laughing about it.

But Terry and Darrell didn't laugh when they read the *Globe* story about their relationship. Months later, Darrell was still bothered by his part. He kept asking himself, "How could I have said that?" Terry told Darrell he couldn't give press interviews any more. Darrell was hurt. The group decided that only Terry and Doug would speak to reporters. "It bugged me for the rest of the trip," Darrell remembered. "It was one of those things that you look back on and say, 'Oh, no.'"

The days continued good and bad. Sometimes the mood depended on whether Terry had been able to sleep the previous night. Most nights he couldn't, despite his new home, a twenty-two-foot camper van that had arrived courtesy of General Motors and Jim Pattison Group, a Vancouver car dealer whose name was painted on the van's side.

Terry had become so well known by this time that when a Sault Ste. Marie radio station broadcast that he was stalled because a spring had snapped in his knee, a local welder jumped in his car to repair the leg. Within ninety minutes, the spring was repaired and Terry was on the road again.

Terry's brother Fred arrived for his vacation and, just as his parents had in Halifax for Terry and Doug, he took time to help Terry and Darrell sort out their disagreements.

These were also days of triumph for Terry. He had been hearing about the Montreal River Hill for weeks. The hill was on everyone's mind. Those who knew the hill's reputation had made the two-mile slope, south of Wawa, a Goliath to Terry's David. They gave him a T-shirt that read MONTREAL RIVER HERE I COME on one side and I'VE GOT YOU BEAT on the other.

Terry ran four miles before starting the long climb which rises above the deep blue of Lake Superior. He ran up the hill without stopping for his usual break. Bill was waiting at the top.

"Is that it?" Terry asked.

"That's it," Bill grinned, and they slapped hands.

Soon after Montreal River there were two trouble spots. He was coughing. It was a light, dry, and brittle cough that punctuated his sentences like commas. He would get partway through what he had to say, then he would cough. It would go away; he knew it would. Then there was the matter of the sore and swollen ankle. He was treating it with an ice pack and continued to run on it.

Inside, he was worried and a little frightened. "Somehow," he wrote in his diary, "I think it will go away on its own." His ankle didn't heal as quickly as his stump. Again he asked himself, "Is it all over?" He worried that he had fractured his foot. He ran on the ankle for three days, although the ice packs neither masked the pain nor reduced the swelling.

Doug decided to call Ron Calhoun in London to ask for help. Calhoun chartered a twin-engine Aztec and Terry was rushed to hospital in Sault Ste. Marie. He had tendinitis, an inflammation of the tendon, a common affliction among athletes. Terry was given an injection and a handful of painkillers and ordered to stay off his feet for thirty-six hours. The news was a great relief to Terry, who had expected a stress fracture, which would have forced him to stop running for several months. He wrote in his diary that night, "Anxious, waiting, hopeful."

Terry rested, then took a bus back to prepare for his next twenty-six miles. He would run a marathon a day for the next four days.

They were glorious days. The weather was bright and clear, the landscape was tall timber and deep water, and his heart was singing because a boy, ten years old and hairless as an old man, was riding his bike behind him as he ran. The boy's name was Greg Scott, and like Terry he had bone cancer. Also like Terry, he had lost his leg and his hair, but he never lost his hope. The two had met in Hamilton, near Greg's home in Welland, and Terry had questioned Bill nearly every day for news of the pale boy who, only months earlier, had been an all-star baseball player.

A family friend, Don Chabot, flew Greg and his parents, Rod and Sharon, to Terrace Bay, a town of three thousand on the shore of Lake Superior, for the reunion. Greg could do a lot of things Terry couldn't. He could ride a bike. And he could swim better than Terry, who had swum only twice in the three and a half years since he lost his leg.

They tested the water in Jackfish Lake with their artificial legs. "Feels nice," said Terry. "It's warm," said Greg, the *Star* reported.

Christie Blatchford, then a reporter with the *Star*, watched from the beach as Boris Spremo took photographs. She watched Greg hop to the water without his artificial leg and dive in effortlessly. She watched Terry unstrap his own leg and wade towards Greg, who sped to his side squealing and splashing. Terry tumbled off balance into the lake, and the whole marathon crew joined in, hooting and whooping its way through the water, like a bunch of kids on any summer evening. They came out dripping, shirts clinging. The film crew of John Simpson and Scott Hamilton were there, too. Shivering on the beach, Terry found a microphone strapped to his leg and he clucked at John for being devious. Then he picked up his leg and shouted to everyone: "Hey, you guys! You never learned how to walk on an artificial leg, did you? This is how you do it." Then he hopped to the van, his leg in his hand, using it as a cane. Later Terry spoke quietly to Blatchford. He looked around to make sure no one else could hear: "Greg's not as lucky as me. He's got it again. They found a spot of cancer again on his lung."

Wednesday, August 27
Day 138

> Today I had a good run in the morning. Thirteen miles. The weather was perfect. No wind and cool. In the afternoon my ankle started to hurt again. Greg rode his bike behind me for about six miles and it has to be the most inspirational moment I have had! The final thirteen were hard but I made

it! At night we had a beautiful reception in Terrace Bay. I spoke about Greg and couldn't hold back the emotion.

Terry had become very emotional. He saw the Marathon of Hope as more than a run; he saw it as a great swelling of common purpose among the people of Canada. He was touched beyond words by those who cheered him, supported his cause, and shared his dream. He could see it in their faces as he spoke. He was borne along by the crowds. The excitement of the early days, the fundraising, the message of hope for all cancer patients, all the basic reasons for his run were still strong, but Terry felt something more profound, which he found difficult to express. He had come close to Canadians through six provinces and sensed that those people, too, wanted to help the world a little and were inspired by his positive example. He did not want to let anyone down.

Thursday, August 28
Day 139
3,255 miles

Today was a difficult day. Extremely hilly and I was fatigued. Two film crews were buzzing around me all day. It was a gorgeous day. Beautiful; glorious scenery. I did two interviews at night and then read the Doug Collins [a New Westminster columnist] paper, which said I rode through Quebec and I nearly blew up! Broke my heart! I have a saddened and weakening attitude toward the media and press.

This is, in part, what Terry read: "God knows, I don't want to take anything away from Terry Fox, B.C.'s Marathon Man. Would I spit on the Queen? . . . No, Terry will not have run right across Canada because he didn't run right across Quebec. And he didn't run right across Quebec because Quebecers showed almost no interest in him. . . . He ran only 150 of the 700 miles from Gaspé Peninsula to Montreal. He did the rest by van, his reception in La Belle Province being so poor, and then he ran around Montreal to complete the equivalent mileage."

Terry, who read every word written about himself, broke down: "I read that story when I was fully exhausted and had given everything I had that day in running; then to see that, it just degraded me and I cried. I burst right down. I punched the wall, and Bill and the others thought I was going to put a hole through it. It just burned me, tore through me. To me it was so important to be as honest as I could, to always tell the truth, and not even to miss a foot."

Terry phoned New Westminster and a retraction was printed. "I don't know," he said later, "if I've gotten over it yet."

Friday, August 29
Day 140
3,275 miles

> Today was a difficult day. I didn't sleep last night and was wiped before I started. Exhausted and fatigued all day. Got a lovely, beautiful poem from Rika that lifted my spirits. I feel sick tonight.

Doug knocked on the cabin door. Terry was soaking in a hot bath. Bill was with his family in Welland. Doug cautiously brought up the matter of Terry's route through Thunder Bay. Lou Fine wanted Terry to run through the city instead of taking a bypass that would save him twelve miles. Terry was worrying about winter. He could already feel the chill in the air. He didn't care about the receptions so much these days. The pressure was on.

Doug had changed since those days in Newfoundland when he would stand still as a post with his arm outstretched with a cup of water. He would never take a day off. "I thought, I belong with Terry."

He was Terry's man and he would not let anyone coerce him into running extra miles. "I thought, to hell with those guys," Doug remembered.

As Terry soaked, the two old friends chatted. It was a quiet time for them. Terry apologized for being so irritable, as though he couldn't comprehend his own anxiety. Doug, in turn, told Terry that he understood how hard it was. "When I started doing the press work I got a better perception of how difficult it was for Terry, and I wasn't even running the miles," Doug said. "Then Terry said he'd probably be bitchy again. But I can't remember if he told me he didn't feel well.

"The next morning it was pouring buckets all through Nipigon. He was sleeping in an extra couple of hours, and it was a good idea because the rain stopped as soon as he came out. He told me he didn't know if he could run because he had the flu. He ran twenty miles that day, Saturday. He wasn't coughing at all.

"The next day, Sunday, he ran twenty-three miles. I told him he had to run fifty-two miles to get to Thunder Bay. There was good weather, and there was no reason he couldn't make twenty-six that day, but he didn't. I thought maybe his foot was still sore."

Sunday, August 31
Day 142
3,318 miles

> Today was all right. Started late and it was cold for the entire morning. Twelve, eleven. Nothing else happened.

Terry had written the last entry in his diary.

11

"DO YOU THINK IT MIGHT

BE CANCER?"

"I had run thirteen miles in the morning and it felt good, it felt real good. It wasn't raining, but it was a cloudy day. Then I ate, as I usually do, and went back to my room – I had a room in a little motel – and slept for a couple of hours. Then I came out and we drove to where I'd left off. By now there were all kinds of people, tons of people, lining the roads waiting for me because the radio stations had been broadcasting.

"I was about eighteen miles out of Thunder Bay. I started running and still felt pretty good. I think it was starting to drizzle rain a little bit. People were clapping me on, cheering me all the way for the whole eight miles that I did in the afternoon. It was super help for me.

"When I finished my fifth mile, I started coughing. I went into the van and I was lying down, taking a drink and a bit of a break. That was my eighteenth mile of the day, or my fifth of that run. I was coughing really hard, and then I felt a pain in my neck that spread into my chest. It was really quite a strong pain. Finally, I got myself to quit coughing, but the pain didn't leave.

I didn't know what to do so I went out and ran because it was the only thing to do. I wasn't going to sit there in the van and wait for it to go away. To me it was like having a blister that I knew would not go away until it had time to heal. As far as I was concerned, the pain in my chest was something that would eventually go away. If it didn't, it would be something that I would have to get checked out.

"People were still lining the road saying to me, 'Keep going; don't give up; you can do it; you can make it; we're all behind you.' Well, you don't hear that and have it go in one ear and out the other, for me, anyway. To me, it goes in one ear and stays there. When I listened to that it meant something to me. Even if I never responded, which I couldn't do all the time, any time anyone said anything to me, I heard. It meant something and probably motivated me.

"Even if I had been by myself, I would have kept going anyway. But I remember that being an important part in the period when I was running – what the people were saying when I had the pain in my chest and it wasn't going away. It was a dull, blunt pain in my upper chest, and it hurt, oh, it really hurt to run, but I kept going, hoping that eventually it would go away or start to fade. After two miles it was getting worse, but my legs were okay and my arms were okay so I could still run. I got those miles done and then I went in the van, took the sleeping bag out and hid in it for fifteen minutes, and hoped that by taking that rest it would go away.

"But nothing changed. The pain was still there, so I got up, went out, and tried again. There were people lined up for about three-quarters of a mile or so. The van went ahead one mile and waited for me. The police car was behind me. And I was running with this pain in my chest and I began to think, you know, there's something wrong. This may be the last mile.

"There was a camera crew waiting at the three-quarter-mile point to film me. I don't think they even realized that they had filmed my last mile. And those comments: people were still saying, 'You can make it all the way, Terry.' I started to think about those comments in that mile, too. Yeah, I thought, this might be my last one.

"I actually thought I had a heart attack. I thought I must have had a slight attack. My breathing hadn't changed; except earlier, the day before, I had noticed a shortness of breath and I thought it was just a cold or something.

"So I ran that mile and got in the van, thinking this might be it. I said to Doug: 'Will you drive me to the hospital? I've got to go, and it's not my ankle, it isn't my foot.'

"So we didn't say a word. I just lay there under the covers. Then I told him I didn't want to go into the hospital right away; I wanted a doctor to come and see me in the motel room. So the doctor from the hospital – he was actually from Newfoundland – came out to see me.

"The doctor checked everything. He checked my lungs, too. He told me what he thought it was, either an infection in the lung or a collapsed lung. He was wrong, though.

"I said to him, 'Do you think it might be cancer?'

"He said, 'I don't know. I don't really know at this point, but I don't really think so.'

"Ha, even though he knew, he had asked me, 'When did you have cancer?' and this type of thing. And then I just knew, I knew it, I knew I had it. We went to the hospital and waited.

"I had X-rays and the doctor came into the room and said, 'You've got a slightly collapsed lung. I can't tell if there is an infection or cancer.' But I knew it. I felt shock, incredible, unbelievable shock. How could this happen? Everything was going so great and now, all of a sudden, it's over, the run's over. I can't run any more. The whole thing's changed. Now I'm going home.

"Then we went to the doctor's lounge and waited while the doctor went to get the opinion of a specialist. He phoned a couple of people and got them to come down to the hospital.

"So I said to the doctor again, 'What do you think it is? What do you really think?' and he said again, 'I really don't know.' So we went in to sit down and I cried. I couldn't believe it, I couldn't believe there was any chance of cancer coming back 'cause I'd done all my research and reading. I had gotten to here and now it was all over. That was my initial reaction. Then, like before, I accepted it and realized there wasn't a thing I could do about it and weeping wasn't going to change a thing.

"Even though it wasn't confirmed, I knew I had cancer. Then I went into another room with two doctors. They both said they weren't sure whether there was an infection or cancer. And I said, 'Come on, you've seen this before. You must have an opinion. You've seen the difference before.'

"Then he said to me, 'It looks like it's cancer.' Then I knew for sure.

"That night I phoned my parents. They weren't home so I phoned Mrs. Alward and asked if she could get hold of my parents, tell them to get home so that when I phoned they'd be there. They finally came home and I told my mom, 'Have you heard?' and she said, 'Well, I heard on the news that you're sick,' and I said to her, 'No, that's not it. I got cancer in my lungs, cancer again.'

"She broke down right away, and Dad got on the phone and he couldn't believe it either. Right away they said they'd come out. Then Doug Vater – he's an unbelievable person; I don't know where he came from or why he came, but he really helped my parents – he came over, perfect timing, and Mom asked him if he could arrange a plane to Thunder Bay for them. He got to work right away on it. They were going to ask to hold the plane, but it would have been for too long a time. So they took the later plane at 10:00, and they got out here in the morning. When they came and saw me there wasn't much to be said, really. When they came in, they both grabbed me. We all cried and that was it.

"Even Darrell and Lou Fine didn't know. They had been running around all day looking for me. I thought Doug had got hold of them or somebody had let them know. But I had to tell them, too. They came in the room and I said, 'Did you guys hear?' I was just kind of joking, almost laughing. I had this unbelievable piece of news to give them, and I just said that I got cancer in my lungs again. Darrell said to me, 'Isn't once enough?'

"He and my dad both say things like that. That wasn't my feeling towards it at all. I couldn't feel sorry for myself, or I couldn't get like those people who say it isn't fair. But how can it be fair, when thousands of other people have the same thing? How could I feel sorry for myself when there's little Greg, or somebody else, right now in a hospital, anywhere in the world, dying of cancer? I felt that people all across Canada were going to be seeing me now. I was not gonna be a big ball of tears and feel sorry for myself and say, 'Why me?'

"I decided I was gonna take it as a new change in my life. I was going to have to accept it and fight it, and if there was any way I could, I'd get back out there and run, that's what I was going to do. That's what I said to myself and that's what I said when I was on TV, too.

"Later, I asked the doctor if I could go out to lunch with my parents and Bill. I didn't want to eat in the hospital. He didn't really want me to, but eventually he agreed. We were walking across the road to our car, and all of a sudden I started to feel incredibly terrible and began to get dizzy. I said, 'I can't go out with you. I want to go back to my room.' So I started to walk back across the road. I made it across then I started to get wobbly. Inside the hospital I started to collapse and they grabbed me. There happened to be a chair there and I ended up in it. I had fainted from it all. The day before I had run twenty-six miles and now I couldn't even walk across the road."

Terry asked the doctor if he couldn't stay in Thunder Bay, take treatment, and then continue running. He wanted to finish his marathon, secondary cancer or not. When the doctor explained he was too ill to carry on, Terry accepted and understood that he had to go home. He was in a great deal of pain. That afternoon, Terry was on a stretcher when he told reporters the news.

"In the press conference it was emotional. I was sitting there and all these people were lined up. I'd come so far. I was nearly two-thirds of the way – and I still don't get recognition for that, damn it – and I'd come through so many hard times, so many different experiences, different weather conditions, times when I couldn't sleep, when the humidity was so bad, and when I had so many things to do at night, times when I nearly got run down. I'd been through so much and I'd made it there. All along I'd said I would never give up, I'd always do my best. I remember saying when I gave that talk to all the executives that I was either going to make it or not going to make it. I remember saying people can live with cancer or can die with cancer and still be winners. I'm sure I said it that time, too, that either way, in this run, I was going to turn out a winner, because I'm either going to make it or if I don't it's because something happened that I can't do anything about. That is exactly what happened and so I felt like I had won. I felt like I had made it, even though I hadn't. And a lot of people told me that, too.

"I knew I could have done the last two thousand miles, if I had the chance. I knew that myself and that helped.

"But at the press conference, they were respectful. They weren't scared to ask questions, but they let me talk and say my own piece to begin with. I was surprised they didn't ask more than they did. I think it was because of respect for the situation I was in, with my parents there, too. I think it showed class – for the media, anyway."

As he spoke, Betty and Rolly were by his side. Betty held Terry's hand. In her other hand she held a tissue. Tears streamed down her pale cheeks. All the lines in her face, around her eyes, those beneath her mouth curved bitterly downward. Rolly's eyes were hard, his mouth taut and grim. They listened as Terry spoke to the sorrowful band of reporters.

"Well, you know, I had primary cancer in my knee three and a half years ago, and now the cancer is in my lungs and I have to go home . . ." His voice fractured into brittle bits as he spoke, but he continued, his voice softer than ever: ". . . and have some more X-rays and maybe an operation that will involve opening up my chest or more drugs. I'll do everything I can. I'm gonna do my very best. I'll fight. I promise I won't give up."

Christie Blatchford was there, flown in by the *Toronto Star*. She jumped in the ambulance with the Fox family to hear Rolly say, "I think it's unfair. Very unfair."

"I don't feel this is unfair," Terry replied. "That's the thing about cancer. I'm not the only one. It happens all the time, to other people. I'm not special. This just intensifies what I did. It gives it more meaning. It'll inspire more people. I could have sat on my rear end, I could have forgotten what I'd seen in the hospital, but I didn't.

"How many people do something they really believe in? I just wish people would realize that anything's possible if you try, dreams are made if people try. When I started this run, I said that if we all gave one dollar, we'd have $22 million for cancer research, and I don't care, man, there's no reason that isn't possible. No reason. I'd like to see everybody go kind of wild, inspired with the fundraising."

Blatchford has written thousands of newspaper stories, but the lead on this story was the one she and many others always remembered: "He gave us a dream as big as our country."

Terry closed his eyes. The ambulance arrived at the airport where a private Lear jet was waiting to take him home to Vancouver and then to the Royal Columbian Hospital. The Ontario Ministry of Health arranged for the charter, which would be paid for by the British Columbia medical plan.

Terry, still strapped in a stretcher, was loaded onto the little jet. There was room only for his parents and Dr. Geoffrey Davis, a Cancer Society medical adviser. There was an alarming build-up of fluid in Terry's lungs, and the doctor was prepared to drain the fluid or order an emergency landing if Terry couldn't be cared for in the air. Bill Vigars was left desolate on the tarmac. He had been in St. Thomas celebrating his parents' fortieth wedding anniversary and had rushed to Thunder Bay as soon as Lou Fine had called with the news that Terry didn't have the flu, as had been reported, but that he had cancer. They had hugged goodbye, and Terry realized in that sturdy embrace how much he loved Bill and what a good friend he'd become.

Over the lakes of Manitoba, the wheat fields of Saskatchewan, the foothills of Alberta, the snowy peaks of British Columbia, the two thousand miles he believed he would run, Terry drifted in and out of sleep.

Bud Bird, a former air force pilot, was at the controls. He'd been planning to stop in Calgary for refuelling, but was told that Terry didn't want to face reporters again. The winds were favourable, so they flew directly. As they crossed Canada, air traffic controllers in every sector asked about Terry's health. When the questions were more than the pilot could answer, he put the doctor on the radio.

Moreover, the controllers cleared all traffic, including jumbo jets, out of their way, so the little jet could take the most direct route to Vancouver. "It was very emotional from start to finish, as word spread across the county," Bird said. "In more than forty years of flying, it ranks as my number-one memory."

Betty wept and talked to Dr. Davis, reminiscing about Terry's youth and the exceptional drive he had always shown. She said she had always been afraid of this day. Terry, lying on the stretcher, was lost in his own thoughts. Sometimes he had fantasized that the cancer would spread to his lungs two months after he finished running. Never in his most desperate moments had he guessed that the cancer would recur while he was running.

In Vancouver, reporters and cameramen waited for the plane to touch down at a small airstrip across the highway from the international airport. At the last moment, hoping to protect Terry from prying cameras and questions, Dr. Michael Piper asked that the aircraft land at an alternative runway.

Darrell and Doug, meanwhile, were on a regularly scheduled commercial flight, coming home. Both felt they had been robbed of the final moments. Both wanted to be with Terry until the last words were spoken at a press conference.

"After being so together for four and a half months, all of a sudden being snapped apart was difficult," Doug said. "I wanted to be there until the end. It wasn't really over. We had to get on an airplane before it was all finished."

In the air, Darrell kept asking the same question: "What are you going to do?" Neither had an answer. Their lives had been bound up in Terry's – his food, his clothing, his water breaks, his speeches, his moods, and his need for them – and now they were adrift, flying to an uncertain future.

Terry, who had always been generous with the media, continued to be, despite the throbbing in his lungs. At the hospital, Dr. Ladislav Antonik, the Royal Columbian's medical director, herded the reporters into a basement room to wait. Terry arrived in a crowded elevator. He was sitting in a wheelchair but, at the door to the press conference, pride pushed him to his feet and he walked in.

He said he would like to finish the run, maybe next year or the year after. He learned that Darryl Sittler was ready to organize the Toronto Maple Leafs and the National Hockey League Players' Association to collect pledges and finish the last two thousand miles for Terry. "No, thanks," he said. He wanted to do it himself.

He said he wasn't disappointed in himself for not finishing this time. He said he was happy with what he had done. If he felt any bitterness it was because some businesspeople had tried to use him to sell their products, but he didn't elaborate.

Betty, still by his side, still holding his hand, was asked how she felt. She tried to say something, and found she couldn't. Rolly helped her: "We've been through this before."

Upstairs, his friends Rick Hansen, Peter Colistro, and Rika Noda were waiting for him. Pia Shandel, a host for "The Vancouver Show," had been following Terry from the beginning and was allowed into his room for a few moments. I was there, too, wishing it was as easy to be a reporter as to be a friend.

I was on vacation in Vancouver and had been in touch with the *Star* all day about Terry. Mary Deanne Shears, then city editor, had phoned early, telling me Terry was sick and on his way home, and that I was to cover the press conference. This wasn't how we had expected it to finish. At the end of the day, I was standing on the sidelines again, this time in his hospital room watching and listening as Terry set the tone – cheering people up again – congratulating Rick and Peter on another championship-winning wheelchair-basketball season. We all dreaded speaking of cancer. So Terry talked about it: "I'm facing it. I'm taking one day at a time. I'm keeping up hope. I'm being positive. I don't want people in here feeling sorry for me. I'm going to be as strong as I can and maybe even get out and do things. I'm hoping the lung condition will improve."

Then he said, "It's one thing to run across Canada, but now people are really going to know what cancer is."

He knew that we had made him a hero and forgotten about cancer. While he said he believed he had beaten the beast, he had never really forgotten that cancer had changed his life and given him a new purpose. Most of us didn't remember that. We saw Terry as hope and courage, a brave soul who took the longer, harder path. We saw an audaciously healthy young man with one leg and, as a song written for him said, the heart of a lion.

While struggling to find purpose in his predicament, Terry realized that the millions of Canadians who had been calling him a hero would now see cancer as the savage disease that it was. Perhaps now the fundraising would go wild, as he hoped. It was September 2 and he had raised $1.7 million – far short of his dream of one dollar from every Canadian. The way he saw it, the Marathon of Hope wasn't ending. The real marathon, that race for his life and the true test of his hope, was beginning.

12

"I WASN'T GOING TO LET IT
TAKE ME THAT EASILY"

Terry wore his Marathon of Hope T-shirt – his favourite one, with the map of Canada and the maple leaf on it – through his first weeks in hospital. He wore jeans and sneakers, too, as if defying his tragedy. He saw visitors selectively. His eyes stayed hard and sullen. Sometimes he would never look up, but keep his gaze fixed on a six-inch stack of mail – a lot of it was pastel-coloured – and talk listlessly about taking one day at a time and about being tired. When he did look into your eyes, with a farewell handshake, there was such fierceness and desperation that words seemed unnecessary. A week before he had been healthy, his world limitless, and his future in his own hands. Already the pink slashes of sunburn across his cheeks were fading; instead there were rings of weariness.

The diagnosis was grim. The tumours had spread, metastasized, to both lungs. In the right lung was a well-defined tumour, the size of a golf ball; in the left, an amorphous, fist-sized shaped lump. It was difficult to know the exact size of the left tumour, which appeared as a haziness on the X-rays, because it was surrounded by so much fluid.

Tests in which cells were removed by inserting a hollow needle into Terry's chest revealed calcium in the tumour, a sure sign that the malignant cells had spread from Terry's knee. Since osteogenic sarcoma tends to lodge in the liver and in the bones, Terry was given a computerized body scan and a bone scan to see if the disease had spread elsewhere. It seemed it hadn't.

Doctors had to explain to reporters that Terry didn't have lung cancer. It was sometimes difficult to understand that Terry had malignant bone cells growing in his lungs. It was reported he had a 10-per-cent chance of recovery.

It had taken a somewhat longer than average time for the malignancy to spread. Most metastases occur within eighteen months to two years after primary cancer, although recurrence is sometimes delayed if chemotherapy is used following surgery. It is not known whether those cells lay dormant in Terry's lungs for three and a half years, or had been slowly growing all the time. Terry's doctor believed the tumours would have been visible in chest X-rays about five months before, although they would have been very small.

Dr. Michael Noble, a cancer specialist, was in charge of the case. He came from a well-known medical family. His father, Dr. Robert Noble, was the researcher who developed the cancer drug vincaleukoblastine, an alkaloid derived from the periwinkle plant, which produced dramatic results in childhood leukemias and Hodgkin's disease.

The tumour in Terry's left lung was too large and parts of it extended too close to his heart for all the cells to be cleanly removed surgically. Terry had to face chemotherapy again. The question was, What drug could he take? He had already had a lifetime dose of adriamycin. If he took any more, the risk of heart damage would be increased. Methotrexate was also ruled out, because of the fluid in Terry's lungs. The drug tends to pool in fluids, and there was a danger it could be released unpredictably and possibly be reabsorbed by the bloodstream.

The alternative was a relatively new drug, cis-platinum, which had been licensed for only one year. It didn't have the same side effects as adriamycin and methotrexate, but did cause nausea. Terry was given the drug intravenously, preceded by a saline solution to maintain a high urine output, because there was danger that the platinum could cause heavy-metal poisoning of his kidneys.

On other fronts there were signs of hope. Isadore Sharp sent a telegram to Terry: "The Marathon of Hope has just begun. You started it. We will not rest until your dream to find a cure for cancer is realized," it read. Sharp proposed that Four Seasons Hotels, with local branches of the Canadian Cancer Society, organize an annual run, to be called the Terry Fox Marathon of Hope Run, as a fundraising event for cancer research. "We will also ask every city and town across Canada to join in on the same day so that you will be running in our hearts and minds every year until the battle is won. Your courage and determination are an inspiration to us all."

The first Sunday in September, Terry lay fully dressed watching the fluids drain from the bottles hanging above his hospital bed into his veins. It was the start of his first chemotherapy treatment and he was rooting for the cancer drugs. The television over his bed was turned on. He watched, in disbelief, the popular country singer John Denver sing a song especially for him. He saw other singers – Elton John, Glen Campbell, Anne Murray, and Nana Mouskouri – sing for him. The Canadian ballerina Karen Kain risked her beautiful neck dancing on a concrete floor for him. She slipped once and carried on.

Terry drifted in and out of sleep. He watched Darryl Sittler, Paul Williams, Gordon Lightfoot, and Ken Taylor, Canada's

former ambassador to Iran, who was hailed as a hero for har-
bouring six Americans in the Canadian Embassy during the
1979 hostage crisis, and the whole cast from the Stratford
Festival's *Beggar's Opera*. The premiers of the ten provinces,
stopped en route to the first and ill-fated constitutional conference, all praised him.

It was the CTV network's tribute to Terry Fox, five hours of
prime Sunday time with local hook-ups from coast to coast,
organized in less than forty-eight hours. Terry saw, in the background of the Toronto studios, blown-up posters of himself, the
famous one where he is huge and brawny, running on a wet
highway on the West Coast. There was also a big tote board
that jumped, according to one report, twenty-five thousand
dollars a minute.

Terry's excitement was ingenuous: "John Denver's doing
that for me?" It seemed that the people of Canada had taken
over where Terry had left off. As CTV president Murray
Chercover said, Terry would see that his "torch will be held."

Terry fell asleep during the broadcast, but later saw the
entire show on videotape. His brother Darrell was with Terry
during the show. "I got the sense he felt so helpless. Those drugs
were going through him and there was nothing he could do.
Sometimes I wished I could help, but I felt fortunate to be there
with him."

By the end of the CTV broadcast, $10.5 million had been
raised. One million dollars came from the British Columbia government for an institute founded in Terry's name as part of the
province's Cancer Research Centre. Ontario announced that a
million-dollar endowment fund in Terry's honour would be given
to the Ontario Cancer Treatment and Research Foundation.
Some big chunks came from corporations. Imperial Oil's president Jim Livingstone donated a hundred thousand dollars on air.
Others, including McDonald's of Canada, Coca-Cola Ltd., Shell

Canada, and Standard Brands, also gave generously. The rest came from the people. September became Terry Fox month in communities across Canada.

A couple of teenagers walked through Toronto's wealthy Forest Hill neighbourhood and collected six hundred dollars for Terry in one afternoon. At Simon Fraser University, faculty and staff raised forty-five thousand dollars in one hour, and the university struck a gold medal in Terry's honour and established a thousand-dollar scholarship to be awarded to a student showing "courage in adversity and dedication to society."

Students from Cloverdale Catholic School in Cloverdale, British Columbia, held a boot throw to raise money. In Quebec City, a bank robber–turned–disc jockey organized a twenty-kilometre march for him. In Kelowna, British Columbia, the Woodlake Old Time Fiddlers held a dance. In Newfoundland, a man offered to skate two thousand miles for Terry. A Montreal pianist offered to hold a Chopin recital. There were walk-a-thons, run-a-thons, stitch-a-thons (stitch a quilt in a bank in Oakville, Ontario, and donate one dollar) and cut-a-thons. Toronto businessmen organized a To Terry With Love day, filled Nathan Phillips Square, and raised forty thousand dollars. Ontario strippers peeled to their G-strings for Terry, which caused some raised eyebrows at the Cancer Society. And in Port Coquitlam, two six-year-olds, Tara Binder and Melanie Ward, sold cold drinks behind a little sign that said, HAVE A LEMONADE AND HELP TERRY HELP THE WORLD.

The outpouring came not only from Canada, but from around the world. Letters arrived from Saudi Arabia and Israel, from Ireland and Malaysia, even from a family of United Church missionaries in Nepal. Terry received hundreds of thousands of letters, some merely addressed, "Terry Fox, General Delivery, Canada." Some letters urged him to try unusual herbal remedies, including a grape cure. Others urged him to use his influence to stop the use of animals in cancer research. The post office said he received more mail than the entire city of Port Coquitlam during the Christmas season. Bobby Orr and his wife, Peggy, flew to Vancouver and had dinner at home with Terry and his family. Douglas Bader, an RCAF hero who lost both legs in the Second World War, wrote Terry, as did Senator Edward Kennedy.

Prime Minister Trudeau sent a telegram: "I was distressed indeed to hear that you are again engaged in a fight with your old enemy. . . . The whole country is pulling for you."

Later that month, Terry was named the youngest Companion of the Order of Canada, Canada's highest civilian honour. Governor General Ed Schreyer flew to Port Coquitlam on September 19 for a special ceremony. Terry enjoyed the ceremony, but was distressed, as always, to hear the citation credit him for completing more than half his run, not two-thirds.

British Columbia Premier Bill Bennett went up to the Fox house and awarded Terry the Order of the Dogwood, the province's highest honour.

There were many other awards, so many, in fact, that some were stacked against a living-room wall. The gifts most prominently displayed, for a time, were the blow-up of the photograph of Bobby Orr scoring an overtime goal and, more permanently, a close-to-life-size double portrait of Terry. The painting, which could be seen by passersby on the street, was done from news photographs by a local artist.

Terry was also named Canadian Press newsmaker of the year and won the Lou Marsh Trophy for his outstanding athletic achievement. The latter pleased Terry as much as any of the other honours, for all his life he had valued athletic accomplishments. "If what I did isn't an athletic achievement, what is?" Terry said. He was glad that the athletic aspect of his run had been recognized.

Those months were the best and worst for Terry. As he told the *Vancouver Sun*: "Both things were going on. One was so fantastically great and positive and the other was about as terrible as you can get." The fundraising, the letters, the cards, the poems, all helped Terry's spirits. However, the cis-platinum was not doing well against the cancer. There seemed to be no improvement. In fact, Dr. Noble said the tumours looked worse. Terry felt a lot of pain in his left side. When he spoke, there was an obvious shortness of breath.

Since there appeared to be less fluid in Terry's lungs, Dr. Noble started him on aggressive methotrexate treatment again, once a week, instead of every three weeks. After the second treatment, Terry lapsed into a nightmarish world of hallucination and pain, what Dr. Noble called "the episode of confusion." Terry did not eat for three weeks. His mouth and throat were sore with cankers, a condition known as mucositis. He lost between fifteen and twenty pounds.

It was October, and Terry was back at home. "I couldn't walk. I was watching television and Mom had to come help me to bed. I was so weak, my bones were next to nothing. I felt I had some kind of reaction in my head. Dr. Heffelfinger came and asked a thing or two. He tried to force me to drink. I just couldn't. Then he gave me an injection of some sort that put me out. The next morning I woke up and I didn't know what was going on. Mom and Dad said, 'We really can't help you here. You may as well go to a hospital.' They called an ambulance to take me in. Mom didn't think I was coming home again. They put things on me to help me breathe on the way there.

"That night was the worst of my life. I was hallucinating. I didn't know what room I was in. It was awful, a nightmare, but I was awake. I couldn't explain it. It was just that this terrible thing was happening. It finally got dark. I'd see a nurse every now and then, just to make sure it was all real, that everything was okay. Mentally I was just lost.

"They did a brain scan, but there was nothing wrong. They parked me out in the hall, waiting for someone to take me to my room. I was lying there all by myself and started thinking, what's going on? I looked at myself, at my left leg and the size of my right leg – you know how big my leg was. I thought, is this it? Am I here for good now? Then I started to remember. I decided I was bored there. There was nothing seriously wrong and I was okay. The lung doctor had told me the tumour in my right lung had shrunk and the left lung hadn't changed, so there shouldn't be anything different. When Dr. Noble checked me I told him I wanted to go home, and he said okay. They got a wheelchair for me and I could barely get into it. Dad had to push it.

"I had decided. It was a change in mental attitude, deciding I was going back to where I had been before, that I would fight it as best I could. I wasn't going to let it take me that easily."

Terry had won another battle.

Noble said the reaction was a side effect of the combination of cancer drugs, painkillers, and an anti-nausea drug, as well as the stress of being Terry Fox. They adjusted the drug dosage and cut back the treatment, and Terry responded well for a month. The right tumour shrank even more.

Terry took advantage of the time to put his house in order. He started cleaning up his room, which was filled with souvenirs of his trip. He appeared in educational films for the Cancer Society and was paid for his work. The man who had by that time raised $18.5 million for cancer research was flat broke, wondering how he would pay for Christmas presents. He gave interviews until he exhausted himself, but he had a lot to say. In a revealing series of stories for the *Vancouver Sun*, Terry admitted he'd been careless in failing to have regular check-ups, and he gave reporters unusual access to his doctors. The result was spellbinding reading. He also spoke of his faith, and admitted it was difficult to tell a roomful of reporters that he believed in God.

He told me he still felt he was "in the woods" and wanted to become closer to God: "I think of the world and what's going on. Because man's gone through history with so much death, killing, stealing, I don't think man can do it on his own. It's obvious what's going to happen on this earth unless man changes. I, for one, need something to grab on to, to hold on to. I haven't been told I'm going to die of cancer. When that happens, I want to have so much faith I won't have any fears at all. At the press conference in Thunder Bay the last question was: 'Is Terry Fox afraid?' Of course, I'm afraid. You'd be afraid, too, if you were in my position. Now, if my doctor tells me I'm going to die, I want to be able to say I'm not afraid."

Terry had fun in those months, too. Sometimes he joined Rick Hansen and his basketball buddies for an evening at a Port Coquitlam pub. One night Terry was asked for ID. The waitress gasped when she saw his name. Moments later a round of drinks arrived at the table. Terry, forgetful of his fame, asked, "Why are they giving us free beer?"

He still dreamed of running: "I believe that God planned what happened. There was a reason for what happened to me in Thunder Bay. Right now I'm going to fight as hard as I can to beat cancer. If I do, if I come back from this and finish running across Canada, it will be the greatest comeback I ever made."

Terry started testing himself again. He had looked at his pitifully thin leg and decided to make it strong again. He drove up to Westwood Mountain to the go-cart track where he had trained the year before. He started walking. The track was a big loop with cut-off points along the way, so he could either complete the quarter-mile circuit or cut off at any of the loops. He was weak, "almost falling over," at the first cut-off, but he insisted on completing the circuit. "I had to go all the way around. That's just the way I am about everything. It's things like that that I love. They challenge me. They inspire me."

Terry had other challenges, too. No matter how much he talked about religion and becoming a better person, he was still cantankerous on the home front. Betty was usually on the firing line, coping with his snappishness. She was careful to gauge his mood before asking him a question. "When Terry gets angry, it's me that gets it," she said. "And when there are other people around, he cuts everyone else out." Remembering what Lou Fine once said in a *Globe and Mail* interview, Betty added, "I could see people getting mad at Terry to the point of punching him in the nose."

Terry was aware of his wilful temperament. Just as he had tried to overcome cancer, he tried to tame his own stormy personality, but it was tough battling his own instincts and upbringing.

Betty was close to tears most of the time, but, as she said, "When you're around Terry, you have to be strong." Terry's stubbornness was only a small part of the problem because, more than anything, Betty believed her family had been dealt too many unfair blows. First her brother Fred lost his legs, her sister Norma was killed in a car accident, and now Terry. Considering all of that, Betty remained remarkably controlled and was the strength in the family. Among the few people she could turn to for support were Alison Sinson, an assistant director of nursing at the Royal Columbian Hospital, and Lynn Bryan, an administrative assistant at the Cancer Society.

She slept on the couch to be closer to Terry's room so she could hear him if he needed her. If he couldn't sleep they'd stay up together. "Thank God for all-night television," she'd say. Rolly was back at work. His workmates in the railroad yard had rallied and each worked a day for him so that he could have a few weeks off when Terry came home from Thunder Bay.

Others felt the strain, too. There were many requests for Darrell to appear at fundraising events on Terry's behalf. He wanted to participate, but Betty kept him at home, saying that if he went to one benefit he'd have to go to them all. Eventually Darrell took a part-time job for a janitorial company to save money for a car and tuition at Simon Fraser University. Betty had convinced him, too, to take on an academic challenge.

Bill Vigars had difficulty adjusting to his job for several months. He took long lunches and often broke down and cried about Terry. Like Doug, he felt lost. The run had ended so suddenly and they had been wrenched away from Terry without warning. Vigars still kept Terry's T-shirt and shorts from the last mile, and he had one of Terry's running shoes in his desk drawer. He tried to convince the Ford Motor Company not to sell the Marathon of Hope van. He kept a tape recorder nearby to play songs that Terry had liked. One of Vigars's favourite was Willie Nelson's country-and-western hit "On the Road Again." "That's Terry and me," Vigars said. One night he sobbed, "I don't want him to die."

Everyone, close to Terry or far away, felt helpless.

At Christmas, the family showed the stuff they were made of. They had never seen so many presents under the tree. They held their usual Christmas Eve open house. The dining-room table was laden with Nanaimo bars, shortbread, and homemade fudge from Betty's mother, Mary Ann Wark. Terry, his skin the colour of porcelain, his features more refined and childlike than ever, sat in the big, comfortable, colonial-style chair, mostly watching, sometimes talking quietly to family friends who sat in a circle of chairs in the living room. His intensity contrasted with the gaiety around him.

Someone told Betty and Rolly they looked well. "Do I?" said Betty, curling her stockinged feet. "Do I?" said Rolly, sceptically. The strain was evident. A friend brought in a two-foot-high bottle of Canadian Club, decorated with ribbons. It had been passed around the Christmas Eve circle for eight years and was to be retired that season. When it was Terry's turn to drink from the bottle, the Polaroid and Instamatic cameras flashed. "Ah-ha," joked Betty's best friend, "I'm going to sell this to the *Vancouver Sun* and people will see what the real Terry Fox is like." The laughter was welcomed.

Terry was coughing again that evening. He wondered if it was a cold or cancer. He left his seat and walked slowly down the hall as if in pain. He had already started unbuttoning his shirt. Without saying good night, he walked into his room and closed the door.

Terry had eight chemotherapy treatments between September and January. His goal was always to get out of hospital after the treatments and return home as quickly as possible. Dr. Noble said Terry was a perfect patient except for one fault: he would say he was feeling fine and well enough to go home even while throwing up. The doctor noticed that patients with a positive attitude tended to handle the chemotherapy better.

After the treatment in the last week of January, the hospital provided a cot for Betty in Terry's room so she could be with him day and night. His condition was worsening. At the beginning of February, Dr. Antonik announced in a press conference from the Royal Columbian Hospital that chemotherapy was not working and that tumours had spread first to Terry's abdomen, then to the lymph glands surrounding the aorta, the artery that distributes blood to most parts of the body. This time Terry and his parents did not face the press.

Interferon, a rare and costly natural substance extracted from living cells in the connective tissue, was the only alternative course of treatment, although its effectiveness against osteogenic sarcoma was still inconclusive.

Isadore Sharp, Terry's long-time benefactor, told the national office of the Cancer Society about an interferon supplier he knew of from his search for treatment for his son. The society sent an initial deposit of fifteen thousand dollars – though it wasn't known how much the overall treatment would cost, since doctors were experimenting with dosages – and a few days later, Terry received his first injection of human fibroblast interferon. The substance was flown to the Royal Columbian, where Terry was treated as an outpatient, his parents always by his side. It was reported that only a miracle could save Terry and the people of Canada started praying for that miracle. Letters-to-the-editor pages ran requests for days of prayer and fasting in Terry's honour. He was sent home with an intravenous feeder and around-the-clock private nursing.

Cancer patients were devastated by the news of his setback, and struck by the irony that the man who had raised millions in aid of cancer research could not benefit from his own labour. Terry had been their inspiration. Now many felt that they had been cut adrift again. To some, the slogan "Cancer can be beaten" seemed bitterly inappropriate. For others, Terry had taken the mystery out of the disease – at least the public knew cancer wasn't contagious – and they were grateful.

Terry continued to balance on the edge of two futures: he could die, or he could recover and finish running. While he accepted the first possibility, he prayed for the second. He saw Rika occasionally and kept reading the New Testament. He prayed. He continued to be stubborn, which was a pleasing quality, considering he was so very ill. The tumours pressed against his abdomen and he retched frequently. He played cards, watched television, was given morphine to kill the pain. He saw his friends and went to matinees when he felt strong.

The interferon treatment was not successful. Terry suffered an adverse reaction and returned to the hospital in late

February. He had surgery to relieve the pressure on his heart, and reporters kept a vigil in the lobby, anticipating the worst. No one counted on Terry's strength. He went home again and rested, watched hockey games on television, and during one he saw a banner strung along the stands that read, KEEP ON FIGHTING, TERRY FOX.

While he meditated on his future, Canadians considered his legacy. More than $23.4 million had been raised: he had realized his dream of one dollar from every Canadian. He had more than doubled the National Cancer Institute of Canada's 1980 research allowance of $15.6 million.

Shortly after the interferon treatment failed, the province of British Columbia announced plans to honour Terry further by constructing a $25-million interferon plant in Vancouver. Interferon could then be produced and supplied on a non-profit basis across Canada.

But the gift he left most of us was not measured in dollars.

Having seen him, we knew something of courage and compassion. To some he became a symbol of unity. Politicians debating the patriation of the British North America Act or the price of Canadian oil were berated by their constituents for not bringing the country together the way Terry had. They had seen Terry run across Canada with the map of Canada on his chest and he'd spoken openly of being a proud Canadian.

Something rare and wonderful happened. We found a new, young Canadian hero among us. His courage was boundless. The world was a better place because he had walked in it. He gave every part of himself with every breath he took. He was selfless. He had a great heart.

He taught us, not so much in words but in the way he lived, about duty, dedication, doing your best, and always being thankful. He could laugh, though we rarely saw the playful boy in him. He worked hard as he ran along the highways. All of us who watched him that summer understood that the best things, the things that touch us to our core and change us forever, come only with enormous effort.

Terry started his run with a young man's joy and energy. He would get out on the road and run. He would show Canadians what a man with one leg could do. He would raise money. He would inspire cancer patients.

But as he ran, it all changed. He saw a deeper meaning in his struggle, one that could be applied to the healthy as well as the sick. He had seen in his own too-short life that one person could make a difference. You didn't have to be especially gifted. You could be as ordinary as the boy who worked so hard to make the Mary Hill Cobras basketball team. All you needed was the will.

Terry knew he was setting an example and that people were watching him and, finally, listening to him. He used a young man's words: "Every one of us is important." "Just look at what one person can do." People did look at Terry and then at themselves and asked: Have I done my best? What have I done for others? Have I lost a dream?

He saw that many of us felt helpless, that we felt we couldn't control our own lives. Terry believed we could. His leg was gone, but he was alive and he was strong. Never forgetting the suffering he had seen in the cancer wards, he pushed himself 3,339 miles to prove what a young man with a great dream could do.

He saw, too, that he wasn't alone. He had seen that many, many others, from the fishing villages of Newfoundland to the shores of Lake Superior, shared that dream. Like him, they wanted the world to be a better place.

13

"SOMEWHERE THE HURTING

MUST STOP"

Terry died before dawn, June 28, 1981. That quiet hour of the morning, when the world was dark and still, had been his favourite. He developed pneumonia and slipped into a coma. His family was with him and held his hand.

Those final weeks were difficult for Betty, Rolly, and their children – there were more external complexities for this family than for others caring for a son in the last weeks of his life. Sometimes they'd find people standing outside their house praying and chanting. They had hired security guards to stand outside their home and Terry's hospital room.

They needed time alone with Terry and with their own thoughts and found there was no time. Someone always wanted to talk to them. They couldn't go to the cafeteria to get a coffee without encountering a reporter. Hospital administrators were calling them out of Terry's room. There were many questions. "I felt we didn't have that time to ourselves," Rolly said.

They felt as they always had: Terry was theirs and it was difficult to share him, even more so in that critical period. "We know we shared him, but he's still our son and we're still sharing him and it's still hard for us," Rolly said. At times, they wished Terry could have died at home, though they valued the medical care he received at Royal Columbian.

Dozens of reporters, who had kept a long vigil in the hospital lobby, filed their stories. Some of them wept. Flags were flown at half-mast on government buildings across Canada and overseas, an honour usually reserved for statesmen. Terry's family retreated home as tributes poured in from royalty and heads of state. Prime Minister Trudeau, addressing the House of Commons, captured the mood of the country: "It occurs very rarely in the life of a nation that the courageous spirit of one person unites all people in the celebration of his life and in the mourning of his death."

Terry, he said, gave far more to his country than his country was able to give to him. "Canadians wanted desperately for Terry to live to win his personal battle against the ravages of cancer. Yet it does not occur to any of us to look upon his death as a defeat or failure. . . . We do not think of him as one who was defeated by misfortune but as one who inspired us with the example of the triumph of the human spirit over adversity."

Then there was the simple eloquence of Canadians who had never met him but felt a natural bond. "It's as if I lost my little brother," a Toronto woman said.

Terry's funeral, with forty relatives and two hundred invited guests, reflected the restraint and simplicity he had shown in his life. Public memorials were held in churches and gyms across Canada, while the funeral was broadcast on network television.

Beneath the yellow cedar arches of Trinity United Church, Terry's former teacher, Bob McGill, delivered the eulogy:

Well, Terry, you met every struggle in life head-on. You always kept the principle in mind that to be successful

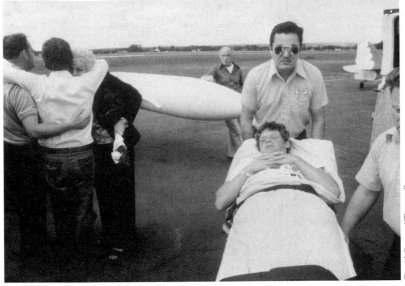

Terry is taken on a stretcher to the plane that would fly him from Thunder Bay home to British Columbia. At left, Cancer Society organizer Bill Vigars embraces Terry's parents, Betty and Rolly.

Terry and his mother, Betty Fox, hold hands during the press conference at the Royal Columbian Hospital in New Westminster, B.C.

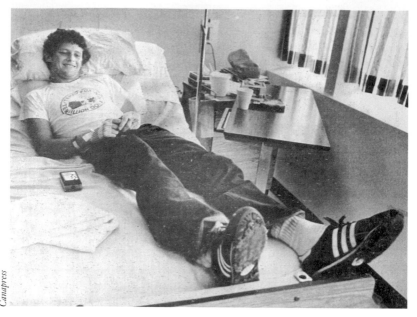

Terry watches from his hospital bed the start of the CTV telethon that raised $10 million.

A Fox family portrait taken on the day when Terry received the Order of Canada. From left to right: Darrell, Rolly, Terry, Judith, Fred, and Betty.

Terry leaves Port Coquitlam City Hall, 19 September 1980, after receiving the Order of Canada.

Participants walk, run, and ride their bikes for Terry in Ottawa,
September 1996.

Students at a Toronto, Ontario school spell out the occasion,
September 1999.

The oldest and youngest participants in the 1998 Terry Fox Run in Bilina, Czech Republic. More than 90,000 people took part in 165 separate events in the Czech Republic in 1999.

More than $35,000 was raised in Mexico City in 1999 through a combined run, gala dinner, and casino night.

More than 10,000 people raised more than $250,000 in the 1998 Terry Fox run in the United Arab Emirates. Canadian Ambassador Stuart McDowall is shown with students about to participate in the run at the Women's College, Abu Dhabi.

There were more than 8,000 participants in the Kuwait City Terry Fox Run in 1998.

An elephant dressed in a Terry Fox t-shirt leads the Terry Fox Run in New Delhi in 2000. The event raised more than $27,000.

Five Benedictine nuns from Kylemore Abbey in County Connemara, Eire, were among the 50,000 participants in more than 100 Terry Fox runs in Ireland in 1999.

Boris Spremo / Toronto Star

The Terry Fox Monument draws thousands of visitors to the spot where Terry's run ended near Thunder Bay, Ontario.

you had to believe in something, really believe in what you were trying to do, setting goals and then working as hard as humanly possible. You've left us a great deal to think about, Terry.

You always loved the challenge. You always loved to do battle, so I know, Terry, you'd want us to keep the battle on. You've passed the torch to all of us, Terry, to keep the fight against cancer on and, Terry, we will not let you down.

At the end of the service, a scarlet-clad Mountie gave Betty a Canadian flag that had flown on Parliament Hill atop the Peace Tower.

Doug was a pallbearer. Now that Terry was free from pain, he said he felt as if a thousand-ton weight had been lifted from his shoulders. In fact, he set his shoulders straighter and seemed stronger and more confident than in the past.

Terry was buried in a cemetery near a lookout where he used to go if he had a problem to think through. The lookout is just outside the cemetery gates, where the road bends sharply and looks over a wooded valley where new housing was encroaching on the forest. This is where he and Rika composed the letter asking for sponsorship for his marathon. "Somewhere the hurting must stop," they wrote. That became his epitaph, engraved on his tombstone, along with "He made his too short life into a marathon of hope and courage."

When the family left the cemetery after the gravesite service, people came quietly and slowly and stopped in front of the mound of earth. They dropped roses from their gardens. A Royal Canadian Mounted Police car stood in the shade beneath the towering cedars and firs. Children silently scrambled over the cemetery fence to look at the grave heaped with flowers. "Sad, eh?" one said.

There was a wreath from the government of Canada, another "from someone you touched in Ontario," and one "to my dear friend, Terry, I love you."

Six weeks later, in Welland, Ontario, Greg Scott died. In a sad, striking parallel, cancer had spread from his leg to his lungs. Frightened of death, he found courage in the thought he would meet Terry in heaven.

In the months that followed, homemade gifts and honours arrived at the Fox door from across Canada and around the world. They were kept under the pool table until the time came for them to be sorted and stored. Thousands of letters and cards were boxed and catalogued by subject – cancer cures, poems, letters from children, religious – and were kept in sixty boxes in a Cancer Society warehouse in Vancouver. The best were microfilmed.

The poems were to be bound in volumes and kept by Terry's family. Of the thousands of gifts and mementoes, the family chose nearly four hundred pieces to give to a Terry Fox library that was built in Port Coquitlam.

Boxes of memorabilia filled the Fox basement. Besides the national awards, there were fifty plaques or trophies, an appreciation award from the Canadian Federation of Pakistanis, Man of the Year from the Canadian Council of Christians and Jews, a plaque from the Country Music Lovers of Lindsay, Ontario.

There were sixty or so framed citations; more than a hundred T-shirts and jerseys, hand-knit scarves, needlepoint samplers, pillows, footballs, baseballs autographed by the Montreal Expos and the Toronto Blue Jays, pennants, buttons, holy water from the shrine at Lourdes, even a teddy bear. More than two hundred amateur composers wrote songs, and two musical scores were written. The family received tapes and records of all of them.

At least fifty guest books were filled with names of mourners who had attended memorial services across Canada. There were a dozen scrapbooks of newspaper clippings and photographs. Many schools dedicated their yearbooks to him and sent copies. And children sent their love with little presents: a used eraser, a pair of a mother's earrings, a pencil stub. Everything was kept.

Terry was known around the world. A woman in Chile sent Betty a tablecloth she crocheted. From China, a writer sent a children's fable based on Terry's life about a one-legged superhero. Toronto philanthropist Louis Mayzel opened a Terry Fox memorial garden in Jerusalem. He vowed Terry would never be forgotten and offered scholarships in Canada and Israel in Terry's name.

Those were the personal tributes. There were public tributes as his name was enshrined from coast to coast, and on land, sea, and air. There was the Terry Fox playground in St. John's. The Terry Fox Youth Centre in Ottawa accommodates 3,200 students who are learning about Canadian life and culture. In Toronto, the Terry Fox House was opened as a group home for young offenders. Schools, streets, and libraries were named in his memory. A fifty-mile section of the Trans-Canada Highway between Thunder Bay and Nipigon was named the Terry Fox Courage Highway. Rising above the highway near Nipigon is a powerful three-metre bronze statue of Terry forging westward. "Even the great pines and granite rocks of the Cambrian Shield are dwarfed by the towering soul of Terry Fox," said Ontario Premier Bill Davis at the opening ceremony.

At Assiniboine Park in Manitoba, a fitness trail with special adaptations for the handicapped was named after Terry. In the Selwyn Range of the Rocky Mountains, a snowcapped 2,639-metre peak was named Mount Terry Fox and can be seen from

the Yellowhead Highway; in Vancouver, there is Terry Fox
Plaza; at Simon Fraser University, there is the Terry Fox Field.
Nordair named a Boeing 737 after Terry, and his family flew in
it to Nanisivik, on Baffin Island, where they dedicated a cairn in
his name. An oil company named an icebreaker after him.

After a vigorous letter-writing campaign, the federal government bowed to public opinion and commissioned a Terry
Fox stamp. Royalty and the Governor General had been the only
living persons who could be commemorated on a stamp; anyone
else had to have been dead at least ten years. Terry, groggy with
painkillers in his hospital bed, heard about the stamp not long
before he died. He is reported to have smiled and said, "I like it."

There were dozens of Terry Fox scholarships, some from the
government. Most prominent were the Terry Fox Humanitarian
Awards, renewable scholarships valued at four thousand dollars
a year from a five-million-dollar endowment fund set up by the
federal government. But the standards of excellence were so
high only eighteen students qualified the first year, although
eighty scholarships were available and nearly two thousand
applied. The awards would go to young people who overcame
obstacles in life – cancer, amputation, poverty, death of loved
ones – and saw beyond their own difficulties to help others.

Terry was named newsmaker of the year for the second con-
secutive year by the Canadian Press and was posthumously
inducted into the Sports Hall of Fame, a reminder that his
Marathon of Hope was also a stunning athletic achievement. He
was mentioned in the 1983 *Guinness Book of Records* as the top
charity fundraiser – $24.7 million in 143 days.

There was a Terry Fox movie and, prompting an eerie sense
of déjà vu, several thousand returned to Nathan Phillips Square
in Toronto to relive Terry's summer triumph for the cameras.
There were actors on the stage, but the recorded voice was
Terry's own.

In the United States, members of the California legislature passed a memorial resolution for Terry. As one legislator said, they felt as if they had lost someone from their own family. And mailman Donald Marrs of Cincinnati, whose cancer of the lymph glands was in remission, crossed the Golden Gate Bridge under a rainbow, ending a transcontinental walk of faith for Terry.

Isadore Sharp, working quietly behind the scenes, kept his promise to organize an annual run in Terry's honour to raise funds for cancer research. Terry had been explicit about what he would and would not approve. He did not want anyone to finish his run for him, nor did he want the proposed runs in his name to be competitive. "He wanted everybody to participate. He wanted something inclusive, where people could run, walk, or ride," Sharp said.

Sharp, the Four Seasons Hotels, and the Cancer Society organized the first runs in September 1981. About 300,000 people running in 760 locations across the country took part and raised $3.2 million. Terry Fox Runs have been held in parks, in city streets, and on country roads on the third Sunday in September ever since.

It wasn't easy to establish – the Fox run was seen as competition for established charities. Sharp had to argue with Cancer Society and government officials that other charities would not suffer in their appeals if a new national fundraising run was held in Terry's honour in September, the month he stopped running. Some said it wasn't fair that the Cancer Society have a second big public campaign – April is the traditional fundraising month for the Canadian Cancer Society. Sharp said that giving doesn't have to be limited to once a year.

"If it wasn't for Mr. Sharp all those years, I don't know where we'd be," said Betty Fox. "He was the one who made it happen. He's really been my right arm and he played such an important role, especially in those early years." For a few months each year a run director was hired in each province to publicize and organize a run, with funds going to cancer research.

Over the years the role Betty and her family played became increasingly important until, in 1988, the Terry Fox Run broke away from the Cancer Society and became an independent foundation.

Terry would have approved of the annual runs – they're exactly the way he would have wished them to be.

The serious runners and sprinters often come early and are long gone before the majority, casual athletes at best, who enjoy the exercise, the conversation, and being outdoors on one of the last days of summer. There's always a wonderful feel to the day, and it rarely rains. It has become a tradition in some families and has been passed down from parents to children who did their first runs in Snuglis, then graduated to strollers, tricycles and wobbly bicycles, and finally were old enough to run on their own. For some it's a challenge to find sponsors and then walk or run the ten kilometres. Some run to keep Terry's spirit alive and some because of Terry's example. While most are able-bodied, it's not uncommon to see people with disabilities – they may be in wheelchairs, using walkers, or visually impaired. Dick Traum, the one-legged marathon runner Terry read about the night before his amputation, came to Toronto to run. The elderly walk their dogs, young parents push baby carriages, women who have never run in their lives get in shape and run for Terry. Corporate teammates, in matching T-shirts but of all shapes, ages, backgrounds, and levels of fitness, run and chat together. Orange-turbaned and fit young Sikhs flash by. In Port Coquitlam, Rolly and Terry's brothers and sister walk or run while Betty works at a table accepting pledges.

There were some letters in the papers from Canadians who objected to the way the money Terry raised was being spent. Some said the funds were being misdirected if they all went to research: What about prevention? they asked. There was no room for argument, since Terry never considered any option but research. As the Cancer Society geared up for its spring fundraising drives, volunteers had to explain that Terry's money wasn't going to the society – and therefore it was not paying for much-needed daily services to cancer patients, such as care for the bedridden – but to the related but separate National Cancer Institute of Canada, the research arm of the Cancer Society. Dr. Peter Scholefield, the institute's executive director at the time, said that, if we're interested in prevention, we have to know what it is we're preventing; if we know what causes cancer, we're better equipped to stop it.

By March 1983, $30 million were marked for research in the accounts of the National Cancer Institute. That included money Terry had raised, $5.5 million raised in two Terry Fox Runs, plus interest. The first year's $4.7 million had already been paid out to the scientists working under Marathon of Hope research grants. Scholefield said it was likely that the fund would never be higher than at that time, would probably start on a downward curve, and could even be depleted within seven to ten years. His prediction greatly underestimated the impact of Terry Fox that continues to this day.

Terry's millions came at precisely the right time for Canada's scientific community, for there had been a crisis in medical research because of reduced funding. Just as Terry turned on Canadians, so he also turned on the scientific community, Scholefield said. The opportunity for research had never been more promising or exciting than in the years after Terry's death.

The problem was how to spend the money. The board of the National Cancer Institute first met to thrash that out the very month Terry stopped running. They held a brainstorming session: Buy gold, one of the board members suggested, and every year offer a million-dollar prize for the best cancer research in the world. Spend it all on interferon, another suggested. Build a national cancer research hospital and laboratory, said yet another.

Dr. Louis Siminovitch, head of genetics at Toronto's Hospital for Sick Children, headed the grants committee to decide on worthy programs. American scientists praised the reasoning and farsightedness of the grant plan the committee developed.

Under the Special Initiatives Program, grants of one million dollars each over five years were awarded to five of thirty-six scientists who applied in the first two years. Canada's most promising researchers were chosen with the hope they would act as magnets and draw other top scientists to their labs. At the Hospital for Sick Children, for example, Dr. Robert Chambers and Dr. Jeremy Carver were studying how cancer cells spread – important research, considering that Terry died after bone-cancer cells spread to his lungs.

The Special Cancer Research Fund was tailor-made for Canada's sixteen medical schools and offered grants of up to $150,000 each over three years to buy or upgrade equipment or fund new research programs.

Training Centre Establishment Grants for hospitals or research centres were to bring promising young medical doctors and Ph.D.s together for their training, combining patient treatment and laboratory research. In 1981, five out of twelve centres that applied were awarded up to a million dollars each over five years.

Research Scientist Awards paid the salaries of top Canadian scientists who would agree to spend 90 per cent of their time doing research.

A Cancer Research Clerkship Program provided for summer jobs in research for first- and second-year medical students. It was hoped that after the exposure to research, young doctors might be able to recognize the earliest signs of cancer in their patients. More than two million dollars was to be awarded over five years.

In addition, a Cancer Research Exchange Program allowed scientists to travel abroad to spend up to three months in another researcher's lab to learn the technology and bring it back to their own labs in Canada. In the first year one scientist applied – to study in Hong Kong – and spent only five thousand dollars.

There was also a Terry Fox Special Awards Program, which included funds for research and special investigations, and a three-million-dollar five-year grant went to the University of Toronto for its national breast-screen study involving ninety thousand women.

This was Terry's legacy, and it was only a beginning. Few could have predicted that many years after his death the funds raised around the world in Terry's name would increase by ten times, and that his message of hope and his shining example would resonate with those who remembered him and with a generation born after his death.

14

"HE WAS RUNNING IN OUR HEARTS ALL THE TIME"

In tiny Paradise Hill, Saskatchewan, Gwen and Richard Zweifel have nine sons and one daughter and a mixed farm where they grow grain and raise cattle. Richard also hauls cattle commercially while Gwen drives a school bus and cooks in a restaurant. Their family has grown up, though they remain close.

Gwen and Richard didn't see Terry run. They didn't see his pain and his struggle, though they were and remain in awe of the vision that drove him across the country.

Because of that, they organize a Terry Fox Run in nearby Frenchman Butte, population sixty-five, every year. Over the years the 150 people who come out regularly have raised more than a hundred thousand dollars in the two communities.

They do Terry Fox Runs differently in rural Saskatchewan than in the cities and towns. Some ride horseback, one family drives a team of white mules, and some canoe down the North Saskatchewan River. "It's not all roses," says Richard. "There are lots of undercurrents."

At the end of the day of running, riding, or paddling, they hold a social with sandwiches and cake. Gwen was shocked at the notion that you'd ask people to bring food. They just do. She hardly thinks of the annual run as the result of organization. "It just happens," she says.

How is it that they could be so moved to work for nearly two decades in memory of a young man they never met?

"It doesn't matter that we didn't meet him, because he was running in our hearts all the time," says Gwen. "It was such a personal thing to think someone who went through what he went through and still had that kind of sincerity and dedication and ambition for the rest of us. The odds were against him and the scope was so huge and still he did it. I can't even grasp the vision he had."

Many families in their area have been affected by cancer, Gwen says. "Our community has been touched so deeply, so many times. When one family hurts, we all do. That's what drives us." Her family has suffered, too. Three of her children have inherited kidney disease: one son has had two kidney transplants, and his sister, who was a donor, is ill herself now. Their eldest son has also had a transplant and is doing well, which gives them some hope. "We know what it is to have illness in the family and face it every day," says Gwen. "Because of that we have a deeper understanding of people who are suffering."

The Zweifels and others like them across Canada and overseas have picked up the torch and become the new Terry Fox story. In the most natural way, the way you put on a sweater when you're cold, they have turned over part of their lives to keep his dream alive. Terry's hopes have become their own.

These people contribute in many ways. Some reach out in their communities and organize local runs; some gather pledges; some make use of their contacts on Bay Street; some work for Terry from wheelchairs; some from prison. In small gestures (those one-dollar pledges that add up), and large (those fat corporate donations), people continue giving.

If anything, the sense of urgency and commitment to help Terry on his mission is stronger now, twenty years later, than it was in the years immediately following his death.

There were 129,300 new cases of cancer diagnosed in Canada in 1999. About 63,000 died of the disease. Everyone has a cancer story to tell. Eleven-year-olds still die after brave struggles against leukemia, and the suffering in their too-brief lives is imprinted on their families and young friends forever. Grandfathers spend the last years of their lives taking chemotherapy treatment, hoping against the statistics that they will survive. Young mothers who are also fierce competitors succumb to cancer, like curling champion Sandra Schmirler, who died at thirty-six.

Against this background, this life-and-death struggle, Canadians have taken up Terry's task, finishing his run the proper way, and the only way he would have permitted. These are extraordinary people, who would describe themselves, as Terry described himself, as ordinary. Some, like the Zweifels, never heard his footsteps in the early-morning dark, but were still moved by him. They are of all incomes and ages, like Riley Simonite of La Ronge, Saskatchewan, and Percy Jordison, of Moose Jaw.

Riley is eight. For his last two birthdays, which falls in September, he has asked his friends to bring pledges for the Terry Fox Run instead of presents. He usually invites his entire school class and, after discussing things with his mother, Barb, concluded that it would be too much to receive thirty presents.

He'd read about Terry and thought, "What a hero." "It's tough giving up presents," said Barb, "but the kids watch the money go into a jar. They think it's awesome."

For his seventh birthday, Riley raised $127.97. For his eighth, $179. Barb said she'd always found Terry's story inspiring, but she truly came to appreciate who he was after she became a mother. "You think, how do you raise such an amazing kid, to have such altruistic values? Then you give your own child a little nudge."

Percy Jordison was born at the beginning of the last century. He's ninety-nine and has never missed a Terry Fox Run. Now retired from his farm, where he grew grain and raised cattle and pigs, Percy has dedicated his runs to his late wife, Bessie. He believes he was given many more years with her because of cancer research. "Without cancer research, she would never have lived," he said. In earlier years he would walk. Now he leads off the run in Moose Jaw and is picked up by a police cruiser and rides to the finish line.

In Prince Rupert, B.C., Jim Terrion, Jr., doesn't need any help getting to the finish line. He is a compulsive walker and, according to a log he has kept, has walked the equivalent of the circumference of the earth three times since 1978.

Jim is deaf. He was still in school when Terry was running in 1980, and followed his progress, keeping a clipping file of articles about Terry. His mother, Faye, doesn't know why Jim loves to walk. "It's something he has to achieve," she said. "He sets a goal and, until he reaches it, he doesn't stop."

In 1990, Jim, like Terry, set out across Canada, though he was walking to raise funds and awareness for the deaf. In one remarkable day, he logged one hundred kilometres. Though he didn't meet his own fundraising goal in his 9,917-kilometre trek, he has been setting records raising money for Terry Fox. From 1991 to 1999, Jim has raised $310,000 for cancer research. In one summer alone, he raised $47,300.

Jim is a maintenance worker at the Moby Dick Inn in Prince Rupert. During the summer months, he works until 3:00 p.m., and then, armed with his pledge sheets, goes to businesses in the town, wordlessly asking for support. He doesn't have trouble communicating: he writes notes or shows his clipboard with pledge sheets. After dinner, he knocks on doors hoping to catch people at home in the early evening. At 9:30 p.m., he goes to the bars, though he doesn't drink, taking pledges until about 11:00. He enjoys being around people.

"He gets everybody in Rupert involved," said Faye, who lives in Prince George. "He's so friendly. He loves everybody and everybody loves him."

He's also persistent. If someone pledges even a dollar, Jim will go back as often as necessary until he collects that pledge. His goal is to raise a million dollars in Terry's name.

In Corner Brook, Newfoundland, Barbara Colford-Connors vividly remembers that April day in 1980 when Terry came to speak to the students of St. Gerard's School, where she was a special-education teacher. Barbara was asked to wait with Terry until all the children were seated in the gym where they would hear him speak. She sat in a stairwell with Terry. She accurately recalls his grey fleece-lined shorts. They were stained with spots of blood from his stump.

"I thought, 'This fellow's not going to make it.' My first impression of him was that he was very unassuming and quite shy. I asked all kinds of questions about his artificial leg and wanted to see how it worked. So he took it off and showed me how it snapped back." The conversation seemed to make Terry more comfortable, and he was more at ease when he went in to speak to the children and again took off his leg to show them how it worked. They were amazed.

In 1990, Colford-Connors went to work at a new school, Presentation Junior High School, and was joined by teachers who had met Terry in 1980 when they were at other schools. They decided a community-service project that would tie in with their religious studies would be a good way to begin each school year. Terry seemed a natural fit, as a role model for young teenagers in a sometimes difficult stage of development.

The school has about 425 children and over the years they have raised nearly twenty-five thousand dollars. "We don't give rewards like T-shirts, not even pencils," she said. It was important for the children to give something to their community and not expect something material in return. Their teachers promised them that "good feeling" you get when you do something selfless for others.

She's called news reporters to ask them to cover the efforts of her students. She was told they weren't newsworthy. She replied that if one of their youngsters committed a crime, that would be considered a news story. Why not report on the positive contributions of teenagers? She got her coverage.

"We just wanted to show that these young people, with all their hormones, can do something nice for their community. We believe the spirit of Terry Fox is in our school."

The children have run in the rain. "The rain didn't stop Terry," one of them said. Another student said, "I came, miss, because I wanted to get that good feeling you said we'd get."

Ontario is Canada's most populous and wealthiest province, and it is rich in stories of devotion to Terry's cause. In 1999, an unusual woman named Eleanor Brown died. She was a dedicated volunteer at the United Church in Havelock, for the Terry Fox Run, and with the inmates at Warkworth Institution, a medium-security penitentiary. At a memorial service in her honour, the prisoners wept for the woman they called Mom.

She suggested to the inmates, who were members of Warkworth's Junior Chamber of Commerce, that they have a charity event and that the Terry Fox Run was a worthy cause. They agreed.

The men earn very little, from $1.00 to $6.90 a day for work as prison groundskeepers, data-entry clerks, storemen, cleaners, cooks, or library assistants. In 1999 they presented the Terry Fox Run with a cheque for $1,600.

Doug Lagossy, forty-four, calls himself a lifer. He prefers not to discuss the fine points of his career in crime. "My criminal history dates way back. Let's just say I'm where I should be." But he proudly relates how he raised four hundred dollars from staff and fellow inmates in the most recent run.

Lagossy describes his heart problems. He says they are so serious he may never leave the penitentiary. But knowing his poor health and that he was willing to struggle the whole day to complete the ten-kilometre run around the prison's track, inmates gave more generously to him.

Why does he raise money for cancer research?

"Ellie asked us to," he said. "Most people are touched by cancer – inmates' children, their aunts, uncles, friends. For me it's the right thing to do. Even I can do a little to help other people."

He said most of his pledges were one dollar or five, or, rarely, ten. A donation of five dollars could easily be a quarter of someone's two-week pay, he said. "It made me feel good to raise that money."

Lagossy remembered that he had a connection to Terry. "I was in Thunder Bay in jail waiting for my sentence when Terry stopped running. He was just around the corner from where I was."

Ontario's Terry Fox Run director, Martha McClew, said that her visit to Warkworth to receive the inmates' donation at a memorial service for Eleanor Brown was among the most emotional of the Terry Fox events she's experienced. "You have a preconceived notion of what these men are like, and then you see them standing before you weeping about what this woman meant to them. She gave them so much hope for what they could be and she made them feel loved."

With all kinds of people, including prisoners, raising money, it seemed only a matter of time before church people caught the Terry Fox spirit.

Shortly after she was treated for breast cancer, Jane Williams suggested that her own St. Joseph's Catholic Church in Ottawa, where she was director of music and liturgy, should raise funds for Terry Fox. In eleven years, the Church Challenge has grown – at one time fifteen churches took part, though it's now down to five – and has raised nearly $243,000. St. Joseph's alone has raised $204,000.

"To me it's absolutely natural that churches look to Terry Fox as a selfless giver unto death. If that isn't a Christian attribute, I don't know what is," said Williams. "He was a real model of how our lives should be lived."

A pledge sheet at the back of the churches allows parishioners to make pledges for the priests. They usually go as a group after the last Sunday Mass on run day.

Volunteers also stand at the back of the church with "loonie tins" where people drop a coin on their way out the door. It's a way of remembering that Terry asked for a dollar from every Canadian.

Jane Williams also played an important part in seeing that the statue of Terry in Ottawa was moved from an unimpressive location, below street level, at the conference centre, to its more prominent site across from Parliament Hill.

Just as Terry's example was imprinted on Jim Terrion, Jr., in British Columbia, who saw that a disability couldn't keep him from doing something remarkable with his life, it had a similar effect on George Walsh, fifty-one, in Thunder Bay, Ontario.

The fact that he has cerebral palsy and is a quadriplegic – with restricted use of his hands – has not stopped George from raising as much as $4,500 for cancer research each year. He sends letters, makes phone calls for sponsors, and finds real pleasure in raising money for Terry. "It's very important for me to do it," says George, whose father died of cancer.

He starts the annual ten-kilometre run, with someone pushing him, at a significant spot – the statue of Terry on the Terry Fox Courage Highway near Thunder Bay – before joining other participants at the official run start.

"It's an accomplishment for him," said his mother, Norah, a retired music teacher. "With his physical disabilities, he doesn't get a lot of that. He has Terry in mind when he does it. Remember, Terry kept going until he died. To someone like George, that's something."

There is another group of Canadians who raise money not only because it's the right thing to do or because they felt some kinship with Terry, but because their hearts have been broken by cancer. Like Betty and Rolly Fox, Joan and Gus Saunders of Kanata, Ontario, have lost a son. Bob was twenty-seven, a stoker in the Canadian Navy, raw-boned and tender-hearted and, his parents believe, as stubborn as Terry. It took a few years after Bob's rapid death from lung cancer for the family to get its bearings. It was then that Bob's sister, Barbara, suggested the family – Joan, Gus, brother Glenn, herself, and their children – do something for Terry Fox. They've never stopped. They write to friends and former colleagues who know their family's story, and have raised seventy thousand dollars for cancer research.

"In the days leading up to it, we are thinking of him so much and how he would have approved of it. Had he lived, he would have been leading a corps of them in B.C. That's a little bit of a healer for us."

And lastly, there are the volunteers who go after the really big bucks, the corporate donors. Mike McClew has led the most successful corporate challenge in Canada. A Toronto management consultant with a big personality – he's clever, irreverent, and charming – McClew has tapped into his network of business contacts to raise $3.5 million since 1982.

When the business of business is finished, he brings up the subject of Terry Fox. "When you've got something you believe in, you don't feel you're being rude by asking people to be involved," he said.

Face-to-face meetings seem to work best. It's not as if he's asking for money. He's asking that the company appoint a couple of people to organize a run in the office. Increasingly, the company will match its employees' donations.

In 1999, Scotia Capital Markets led the list of Ontario's corporate donors, raising $85,000. But right up there, among the top ten, which included national and international companies – Four Seasons Hotels, Andersen Consulting, Scotiabank, RBC Dominion Companies, and IBM – is a little five-chair beauty salon, Antonio's Touch of Magic, located in a North York plaza. The salon's proprietor is the gentle and modest Joseph Aprile, whose ambition to raise money for Terry is matched by his passion to eradicate grey hair from the world. One of his keenest fundraisers is Mary Deanne Shears, the straight-talking managing editor of the *Toronto Star*, who takes a week of her holidays every year to raise funds through activities like book and bake sales, and barbecues, for Terry Fox. "He changed my life. He started off as a news story and it touched me more than any other because of his grit and the hope we had for him and what he stood for."

In 1999, the little salon that could raised a remarkable $32,189. This speaks to the heart of the Terry Fox Run's success: these Main Street businesses are as important as Bay Street corporations.

It was on a downtown Toronto street that Breeda McClew, Mike's wife, first saw Terry in July 1980. Their daughter, Martha, had been reporting nightly on Terry's progress across Canada. Curious to see him, Breeda took her two young sons downtown.

"I can still see how he looked," she said. "Wonderful, so deeply tanned, his good leg so strong. I didn't even notice his artificial leg. And when I saw him run, I started bawling. It was one of the greatest moments of my life and the boys, my sons, were saying, 'Stop it, stop crying, or we'll never come anywhere with you again.' What I saw was what I hadn't seen on television; I saw the hardship in running."

She also saw in Terry a role model for her four children. "I thought we were the luckiest family in the world to have Terry Fox come on the scene when our children were growing up. He came at a time when we were starved for heroes."

Everyone in the family volunteered. Breeda became national director for the Terry Fox Foundation, and now is international director for the runs.

Just as there were Terry Fox Runs in Canada throughout the 1980s, wherever there were willing organizers overseas – usually posted at Canadian Forces bases, Canadian embassies or high commissions, or working for Four Seasons Hotels – there were international runs. They were hit-or-miss propositions depending largely on the enthusiasm of the local organizer until Breeda went to Ottawa in 1991.

She contacted the Department of National Defense and the Department of Foreign Affairs to ask for help in contacting Canadians working abroad in various capacities. She was given a book, *Canadian Representatives Abroad*, and it became her definitive source for reaching out to the world.

Breeda, effusive, affectionate, making all around her feel loved and important, wrote to every Canadian diplomatic mission and armed-forces base around the world. Who could resist Breeda, with her lovely County Kerry accent, her love of Terry, her harmony with his ambitions? She packages enormous boxes of T-shirts, posters, videos of the documentary *I Had a Dream*, and other materials about the Terry Fox Run and sends them, via Ottawa's diplomatic mail service, to Morocco, to Costa Rica, to Bali – wherever Canadians are posted, including those on peacekeeping missions in violent and dangerous parts of the world.

The growth of the international runs is a staggering success story. In 1992, $800,000 was raised in thirty-two countries. In 1999, 300,000 people in fifty countries raised $5.5 million. Funds raised yearly have increased seven-fold since 1992. Most of the money raised stays in the host country, provided it has both a cancer institute and research program approved by the International Union Against Cancer in Geneva and vetted by the National Cancer Institute of Canada and the Terry Fox Foundation. The run must also be a stand-alone event, not tied in to another fundraising program.

Long-distance runs are commonplace in Canada, but not in other locations around the world. In many countries, such as the Arab states, a Terry Fox Run is an unusual event. People are at first curious, then are drawn along by the spirit of the run.

There are other reasons why people in distant lands have listened to the story of a young Canadian who dreamed of running across his country. Cancer knows few boundaries. His message is similarly boundless – the hope that cancer can be beaten. He imprinted this message with his every step. "He ran to stamp this disease into the ground," Breeda said. "He was more touched and saddened by the suffering of others than his own suffering."

Each relates to Terry in his or her own way. In our wired world, Internet browsers visit the Terry Fox Foundation Web site (www.terryfoxrun.org) and write their own reactions. "Bravest man ever," reads one entry, unsigned. Others write from Abu Dhabi and China. Rev. Noel Baker in the United Kingdom wrote that he had many times told the story of Terry Fox as an example of the kingdom of God breaking into the world.

Terry also faced emotions we all struggle with and hope to overcome – anger, frustration, disappointment – and yet he triumphed. You could understand his courage, devotion, and idealism in any language. He could be as much of a hero to a youngster in Beirut as in Burnaby.

Today there are runs in places from Australia to Zimbabwe. In Singapore, $574,080 was raised in one year. In Ho Chi Minh City, $12,533. In the Czech Republic, ninety thousand people took part in Terry Fox Runs in 1999; even more are expected in 2000, when there will be more than 216 different run sites. Interest in Terry Fox has exploded there. Seven years ago they knew nothing about him, but as the tireless Breeda sent information, people watched the documentary, celebrities became involved, the Canadian embassy in Prague teamed up with Sokol, a national sports organization, and the League Against Cancer, they learned, and Terry became a hero to them.

"It just clicked. The first year forty ran in Prague, the second year two other towns joined. Every year it doubles," said Lucie Cermakova, press and public affairs officer at the Canadian embassy. People always want Canadians from the embassy to come to their runs, she added. There are so many requests, the ambassador, Ronald Halpin, could keep himself busy going only to Terry Fox events, she said.

There was a tiny, poor town in the mountains, Jesenik, where floods destroyed homes, Cermakova said. Though times were difficult, they still held their Terry Fox Run as planned. No one told them they had to.

In Guyana, the Terry Fox Run was front-page news, as three thousand took part, including the nation's seventy-nine-year-old president, Janet Jagan. In Mumbai, the former Bombay, three thousand children were among the six thousand participants. In Abiqaiq, Saudi Arabia, Canadians ran with runners from around the world – Jordanians, Syrians, Egyptians, Australians, and Pakistanis. It was important to show students, especially, real-life examples of heroism, said teacher Douglas Catanzaro.

There are runs in the poorest countries of the world, including Bangladesh, where Betty Fox and Breeda visited a run. They went to hospitals and saw cancer patients lying on the floor, crying for help. "It was the first time I understood the magnitude of what Terry had done and I understood why Terry was meant to do what he did," Betty said. "In this poor country, five thousand people raised a lot of money [$52,000 in 1997], though they had nothing themselves."

There were runs in the ruins of Beirut and in the Golan Heights. In Damascus, women ran in hijab while children Rollerbladed around them. When he read about the run in Damascus, Neil Stephenson, a young Canadian lawyer who was working in the United Arab Emirates, organized one in Dubai. He gained the support of a sheikh in the royal family, placed Terry Fox signs on billboards on the tops of buildings, and in its first year raised $375,000. It wasn't unusual for the Canadian ambassador to congratulate local organizers, as Stuart McDowall, former ambassador to the United Arab Emirates, did, saying they had done more to raise Canada's profile than anything the embassy could possibly have done. Breeda puts this idea a different way: "Terry Fox is Canada's greatest ambassador." In Connemara, Ireland, Benedictine nuns from Kylemore Abbey ran in their long habits, contributing to the two million dollars raised in Ireland since 1993.

In New Zealand, in the most southerly reaches of the planet, more than two dozen police officers from the Otago/Southland region ran several thousand kilometres, visiting eighty schools and talking about Terry Fox. In one of the small schools in a suburb of Dunedin, the principal erected an enormous memory board so that children could pin on it the name of someone very close to them who had died of cancer.

The board was full.

15

"CANCER ISN'T A MYSTERY
ANY MORE"

In the cramped and cluttered offices of the Terry Fox Foundation, boxes are stacked on boxes up to the ceiling. The place resembles a storeroom more than the national office of a foundation that has raised more than a quarter of a billion dollars for cancer research and awarded $16 million in research grants in 1999.

This is where Darrell works now. His title is national director of the Terry Fox Foundation, but what he's doing is fulfilling his brother's dream.

It's been a long road for Darrell from his perch on the van, holding the door open to protect Terry from the wind, to this job with complex responsibilities and where, more than anywhere else, he is known as Terry's brother. Darrell doesn't talk much about the painful five years following Terry's death. He didn't talk about Terry or the run in those years at all. That wasn't the way the Terry Fox story was supposed to end. "Never in my wildest dreams did I think it would end that way. I thought he could beat it. I thought he was invincible."

When his parents took a trip to the Arctic, Darrell stayed in southern Ontario and retraced Terry's route towards Thunder Bay. They tried to talk him out of the trip, but let him go, hoping it might help him through an unhappy time.

He enrolled at Simon Fraser University, took over Terry's scholarship through a special arrangement, studied kinesiology, but didn't finish. He worked in Nanisivik for the summers, doing geological surveys in an iron-ore mine. He competed in the Midnight Sun Marathon and won it one year. He attended events in Terry's honour, but felt uncomfortable. He said he was always grateful to his mother when she said any decisions made about Terry's legacy were family decisions; the truth was, Darrell chose not to be a part of those decisions.

Betty remembers those years differently. That was a time when she leaned heavily on Darrell, who was still living at home. "If there was a problem, I was able to sit down and talk to him about it. He was the one. He was very, very helpful."

He took a job as a bellman, then became doorman at Vancouver's Pan-Pacific Hotel, which had a five-diamond rating from the American Automobile Association. He enjoyed his work and speaks of it with pride. When he put on his uniform, he felt he was on stage. He was playful again, happy serving people, and he was well paid. He was named employee of the year and began to feel confident that he had accomplished something on his own. It took all those years to come to grips with the trauma of losing Terry and to recognize his own place in the world. "Then I was prepared to become Terry Fox's brother."

In 1990, Darrell made a difficult decision. He gave up the job he enjoyed – he said he needed a challenge – and altered his life's path by going to work for the B.C and Yukon office of the Terry Fox Foundation in Port Coquitlam, a job now held by his brother Fred. In 1994 Darrell came to Toronto as assistant national director to Breeda, and two years later became the national director.

With his wife, Bonnie, he has two small children. He was over his head the first few years, he says, but today his eyes shine when he talks about his work. "I will always be inspired by what Terry did," he says. "That will never change."

He reads Terry's words over and over again, looking for deeper meaning. "Did he see something ahead?" Darrell also personally answers every e-mail sent to him. There are no form letters.

As the parents of Terry Fox, Canadian hero, Betty and Rolly had many invitations to speak or visit across the country. They were busy, distracted, had decisions to make, and their mourning was delayed. "The first six months after Terry's death, I don't think any of us realized he wasn't going to be here any more," Betty said.

They travelled to the Northwest Territories, to St. John's, to Thunder Bay to open Terry Fox paths, schools, and playgrounds and to unveil statues. Rolly fought his natural shyness and spoke (nervously, he said) from prepared texts. Betty proved to be an adept and natural public speaker.

They loved these public occasions. They were proud to carry on where Terry had been forced to stop. They believed Terry would have wanted them to continue to play a part so the spirit of the Marathon of Hope would not be forgotten. They were invited aboard the Royal Yacht *Britannia*, when the Queen and Prince Philip visited Vancouver. They bubbled with happiness and laughed that it was over with so quickly they couldn't remember what was said. Since Betty quit her job she had more time to devote to the Marathon of Hope and the Terry Fox Run, but she disliked the lonely nights in hotel rooms and couldn't wait to get home.

As the pace slowed and Betty found more time to herself, she began to relive the marathon from its first days. She wasn't immobilized by grief or her memories, but the second year after

Terry's death was more difficult than the first. She cried when she spoke of Terry and the past, though she was clear and confident when discussing the future of the Terry Fox Run and her work to keep the Marathon of Hope alive.

Betty and Rolly went to the cemetery every week. They made sure there were fresh flowers on Terry's grave. The visits were like quiet times with him. As she watered the flowers, Betty said, "I'm talking a mile a minute under my breath to him. I say I miss him. I tell him what we've been doing. I say I hope what we've been doing is what he wants." She often wished that Terry would tell her what to do.

Sometimes in those early years they wished they could walk away from the Terry Fox phenomenon. Betty disliked controversy but sometimes found herself embroiled in it. When the design of a Terry Fox memorial at B.C. Place in Vancouver was unveiled, she was asked for her opinion. Betty always speaks her mind. "Being outspoken and honest, I said none of us cared for it," she said. The inside was beautiful, she said, but she didn't like the outside tower. Others agreed with her. "The public didn't like it as well."

There had been some ill feelings among Cancer Society staff members, too, and talk of jealousies and resentments. These tensions troubled Betty. Nor would she tolerate anyone claiming a special connection with Terry or those who used Terry's name to promote themselves.

Following the rules that Terry laid down years before, his family continued to be strict about the use of his name and insisted that they be consulted in all cases. People wanted to sell Terry Fox spoons, T-shirts, and lapel pins, but his family always said no to any commercial proposition. "Sometimes even people close to us think we're doing this for ourselves. We couldn't do this for ourselves."

Despite the strain, the publicity, the stares in supermarkets, the occasional conflict, they knew they could not walk away from Terry's legacy. The Marathon of Hope had been the focus of Terry's life and was becoming the focus of theirs. It was now their job to keep it alive, not only because of Terry, though he was certainly the most important reason, but also because they believed they had to help find a cure for cancer.

As the years passed, Betty continued travelling the country, speaking at schools – often three or four a day – and reaching as many as one hundred schools in six weeks. Pushing herself to her limit, she contracted pneumonia on one long tour and arrived home seriously ill. She was taken immediately to hospital where she remained for two weeks.

Isadore Sharp understood early on that the future of the Terry Fox Run lay with children and went to speak to Ontario's minister of education about organizing Terry Fox Runs in the schools. Now as many as 3,500 schools across Canada hold a Terry Fox event each year and one million children take part.

On the tenth anniversary of the Marathon of Hope, Betty and Rolly retraced Terry's footsteps across Canada. They visited the schools where Terry had spoken and homes where Terry had stayed. People remembered what chair Terry sat in and what they fed him for dinner and showed his parents where he slept. "These things were so important," Betty said. "I wondered how far Terry would have gotten in those provinces without all those wonderful, wonderful people who helped keep his strength up and acted as moms and dads for just a few hours."

They were in awe of what Terry had done. How had he managed to visit all those people, make speeches, attend school assemblies, and still run a marathon a day?

"I think what kept him going was a power greater than any of us," Betty says today. "He was given to Rolly and I to raise and was destined to do what he did. I believe that in my heart. I couldn't have said that twenty years ago."

With Betty away several months of the year, Rolly, who has retired, manages their home office in her absence and, when required, goes on speaking engagements or school visits. He still finds public speaking difficult. It's not in his nature, yet he does it. "I'm so proud, I'm so proud of being Terry's father."

His views on Terry's death differ sharply from Betty's. "I don't understand, if there is a God, why he would take somebody like Terry, when there are so many bad people in the world. Terry had so much to live for and was such a good person. You asked me if I was bitter. I was and I still am. I'd rather have Terry here."

All of them have had to reconcile the public view of Terry Fox as untarnished Canadian hero with the Terry they knew, a brother and a son, human, flawed and beloved.

Fred was grown up and away from home when Terry was in training. He visited him on his run in Toronto and later in Wawa with his future wife, Theresa, but until then had never really watched him run. It was shocking for Fred to see the effort and strain. Mostly he was amazed by the selflessness of what Terry was doing.

A father of three, Fred had been working at an oil refinery before taking the job with the Terry Fox Foundation in B.C. Like Darrell, he had much to learn about running an office. There was something else he learned. "Only when I took this job did I realize the impact Terry had on other people. It's still difficult to see Terry in any way other than as my brother – the boy I grew up with and played with. We'd go inner-tubing down the Coquitlam River. We'd pick blueberries to pay for new bikes or our first set of golf clubs."

He is surrounded by Terry at his work. "I'm here to continue what he started. I also have to separate my relationship with

Terry as brother from what I do in my working life. He is my brother and it's difficult to know him as a hero, the way other people do." Fred continues to speak of Terry in the present tense, as do other members of his family.

Judith went to Terry's high school, where there were portraits of him in the gym and at the main door. Judith's most difficult time was September, during the Terry Fox Run, when the halls were filled with posters of Terry, videotapes of the run were shown, and her classmates were full of talk of Terry. She told her mother she wished she could stay home that week. "It's rough on all of them, but she's the only one who will talk about it," Betty said.

Now married to Dale Alder, Judith is a mother of four and works part-time in a community centre. "I still find Septembers hard, even though they are such wonderful times, when people get together in Terry's name and raise so much money. I usually talk to a few schools. It's a huge anxiety thing – I don't want to cry, but mostly I do."

Doug Alward went back to university, thought about becoming a teacher, and decided he didn't have the outgoing personality necessary for the profession. He's a health-care worker at Riverview Hospital, British Columbia's largest psychiatric hospital. He believes he will remain single. He's become a serious runner again, doing a twenty-mile run and several ten-mile runs each week.

He joined a church he'd picked out of the phone book. He was shocked when the first person who befriended him at the church was later diagnosed with cancer. The disease spread, the doctors stopped chemotherapy, and the future looked grim. Doug prayed for his friend and helped him financially. He saw that life had come full circle. He remembered how a woman in Ontario had wanted to help him after the run, when he was broke and didn't have enough money for university fees. He'd told her he couldn't accept anything, but she insisted. It was his turn now to help someone in need. In fact, these discreet acts of generosity were not uncommon. His friend made a full recovery.

Sometimes Doug sees Terry's story from a spiritual perspective. "The whole thing is miraculous," he says. "God selecting Terry for his destiny in life. I think God planned it. I know he doesn't want people to get sick, but God will use tragedy to bring something good, and Terry knew it was something phenomenal."

Often Betty, Darrell, and Doug, too, will say they feel as if Terry is still with them. "At all times," says Darrell. "It's hard to describe the feeling, but it gives me confidence in making difficult decisions. Sometimes I feel that he is close, there's a warmth that I feel, particularly when I really need him. As time passes the closer I get to him, I'm looking for more, for more stories, the words Terry spoke. You could tell me a story about Terry a million times, and I would never tire of it."

Rika Noda, now married to Duncan Schell, is the mother of three small children whom she home-schools. She has attended the same Baptist church for more than twenty years. She lives close to the East Vancouver neighbourhood where she was raised. She finds it difficult to speak of Terry, though you sense her wish that instead of embarking upon his journey, he had stayed home, protected and loved. "I try not to think about it too much. It was an extremely painful time in my life, a very lonely time. I knew I was just a girlfriend, not a family member, but I felt I was on the outside."

For her, the greater legacy of Terry Fox is not the money raised for cancer research, but inspiration. "The real beauty of the story is that he set out to raise funds for cancer research and he did a great thing. In his innocent way, he gave more to people than he was aware of. He made people really think that ordinary people can do something extraordinary. He moved a whole country, but that was not his intention. Inspiration was a greater thing than finding a cure. It compelled people to go forward and to have hope."

Bill Vigars left the Cancer Society in 1983. He reinvented himself several times. He's been a fundraiser for a Toronto hospital and worked for the Ontario Lottery Corporation. He was a cook on a recreational fishing boat in the Queen Charlotte Islands and communications manager for a B.C. provincial ministry. Most recently, he's been a publicist for a television crime series. His second marriage ended.

"I'm one of those guys whose phone number you write in pencil," he says. "I like challenge and adventure."

Over the years, the Terry Fox Run has become the largest single-day fundraising event for cancer research in the world. In 1999, 1.5 million people ran, walked, cycled, exerted themselves in many different ways in Terry Fox Runs to raise $17.9 million.

As the run grew each year, Terry's parents, together with Isadore Sharp and Mike McClew, were certain they could do a better job if the run had its own full-time staff, and they believed they could reduce operating costs, which were high, about 30 per cent of funds raised. They had been using a seasonal staff who worked out of Cancer Society offices in the months around the Terry Fox Run.

They were right. After the Terry Fox Run parted company with the Canadian Cancer Society in 1988, the new Terry Fox Foundation flourished. Operating costs dropped to 22.3 per cent in 1990 and to 12.1 per cent in 1999, a figure considered impressively low in fundraising circles. Break this no-frills management down further and you see that administrative costs are 2.2 per cent and fundraising costs – developing, printing, and distributing promotional materials – are 9.9 per cent. In the same period, the funds raised increased at an average of 13.4 per cent each year.

To put it in a broader context, the Canadian Centre for Philanthropy surveyed three thousand registered charities in the mid-1990s and found that, on average, fundraising costs were about 26 per cent. They did not examine administrative costs.

Darrell is obsessive about keeping costs down – that explains the crowded little office where he works – so that out of every dollar donated nearly eighty-eight cents goes directly to innovative cancer research. That obsession goes directly back to Terry. "Terry gave everything to eradicate the suffering cancer causes," he says. The staff of twenty-one and the volunteers who work in eight provincial offices share that view. Though there are 5,500 Terry Fox events held each year, organizers are not allowed to incur *any* costs. The foundation provides posters, pledge sheets, and the like, but extras – juice boxes, oranges, hot dogs – have to be donated.

The foundation refuses to allow any commercialization of the run, so you will not see the name of a corporation tacked on to Terry's. Most charitable organizations aggressively seek and accept corporate sponsorship, so much so that the line between charity and self-interest has increasingly become blurred.

Refusing corporate sponsorship sets the Terry Fox Foundation apart, says Patrick Johnston, president and CEO of the Canadian Centre for Philanthropy. Because of that principle, the foundation refuses offers of tie-in sales, where a percentage of sales – say for every hamburger sold – would go to the Terry Fox Foundation. They've received and refused offers, for instance, to put an image of Terry on a long-distance calling card.

Darrell remembers that, even when he was running, Terry told his mother, "Already they're trying to exploit me."

"It was amazing at age twenty-one to have that vision and understanding," Darrell says. As for the corporations: "They want to give, but they want to sell their product. It's not genuine. They sell more product and gain a profile because of their association with the foundation, and we're not prepared to go that route. If they want to support the foundation, we'd encourage them to make a donation."

Betty believes if she hadn't been hard-headed in the early 1980s, saying no to projects that were not in the spirit of Terry's original run and yes to good ideas that were, there would be no Terry Fox Run today. "I'm sure there would have been some commercialization, and I wouldn't have allowed Terry's name to stand."

Two decades after his death, people in Canada and around the world continue to be drawn to his story. There had been none like him in living memory, and though others have run similar races, none have had the spirit that set Terry apart. For his family, nothing has really changed. In 1980, Canadians recognized his honesty, hard work, and the way he never lost sight of his goal. Twenty years later, they still recognize and value those qualities. Terry spoke of fundamental truths and simple hopes: cancer is a ravening disease that reaches into the lives of most families; if we work together and share a dream, we might be able to stop its progress; even the most ordinary among us can do something wonderful with our lives. In his running and in his words – speaking from the heart as he did – he made an emotional connection that few could resist.

And that is true, but Rick Hansen says there is more at work. There is the power of the original story that transcends borders, the riveting story of a great champion, and, he adds, there are also those who move the story forward. His family – Betty, above all – has done that.

We can't underestimate the role Terry's family has played in keeping Terry's dreams and ambitions alive, nor the importance of astute advisers such as Isadore Sharp and the McClew family. The match has been perfect and has contributed in countless ways to the success of the institutions that are Terry's legacy.

"It's not an angel in the sky making this happen," says Connie Eaves. "There's reality on the ground, and that is his family, and his mother in particular." Eaves has seen that reality first-hand. In 1980 a gift of one million dollars from the province of British Columbia to the Marathon of Hope (with additional funds raised elsewhere) was used to renovate an old bakery and equip 1,800 square metres of laboratory and office space. It was to become Vancouver's new cancer-research unit, and Eaves, with her husband, Allen, were in charge. It's called the Terry Fox Laboratory and now has a staff of more than one hundred, with forty students and post-doctoral fellows.

Betty has shown the same determination as her son. "The spirit of that family is phenomenal," says Eaves, now a senior scientist and deputy director of the Terry Fox Laboratory, "which is why Terry is what is he is. This not a chance event – these are the genes in the family pool. Betty Fox is an extraordinary person, down-to-earth and unassuming, until you see her drive, going all over the world to keep the story alive."

Yet, there is more than merely keeping a story alive. In those brief few months he ran, Terry affected the way people with disabilities looked at themselves, he forced people to look at cancer and understand it, and perhaps more than any other single Canadian, he changed the vocabulary around cancer, from *victim* to *survivor*.

For two decades, the millions of dollars raised in Terry's name have given Canada's leading scientists the means to focus on cancer, to understand at the most fundamental level how the disease works, how it spreads, and how it can be treated. These funds continue to be distributed to Canadian research institutions, hospitals, and universities by the National Cancer Institute of Canada. Of the institute's fifty-million-dollar research budget, a significant portion comes from a single source: sixteen million from the Terry Fox Foundation.

The effect of the sudden infusion of funds available to cancer researchers in 1980 was electrifying and was felt years later, even by those who didn't themselves get grants. There was a sense that great things were going to happen in Canada. And since the competition for Terry Fox grants was subject to peer review, chances of favouritism were vastly reduced. Furthermore, since Terry represented youth, the programs were designed to attract young people to the field and, as Eaves said, ignite them early.

Since many of the investigations were aimed at acquiring an understanding of how normal cells turn into cancer cells, which requires, in turn, an understanding of the fundamentals of cellular genetics, it took a decade or more to see the fruits of research that began in the early 1980s.

Today, scientists say the insight they have gained into the nature and causes of cancer in the last two decades is unprecedented in biomedical history. The National Cancer Institute describes this as an era of boundless optimism and promise.

In 1980 Eaves and her group were virtually unknown; now they have an international reputation. Terry Fox funding has allowed them and other researchers to become leaders in their field.

Eaves's group has been looking at the genetic changes that occur in cells to make them malignant and cause leukemia and other diseases. Their observations in the early 1980s have led them from the realm of pure research to create a clinical program in bone-marrow transplants. They found, for example, that if you put leukemic stem cells (undifferentiated cells that give rise to various kinds of blood cells) from the bone marrow in an incubator, they disappear; if you do the same with normal stem cells, they survive. This led researchers to surmise that leukemia patients might benefit from donations of their own bone marrow, or autologous transplantation.

In 1998, Darrell announced a new cancer research program called the Terry Fox New Frontiers Initiative. The foundation would provide thirty-six million dollars to Canadian cancer researchers over eight years for innovative and high-risk proposals that might not be funded in the competitive climate of the time. The winning proposals were expected to link researchers with different skills and to achieve groundbreaking results in three to six years.

One of those grants was given to a team led by Linda Pilarski at the University of Alberta in Edmonton to find a new treatment for multiple myeloma, a cancer of the bones and bone marrow, that kills within a few years of being diagnosed. They plan to test anti-cancer drugs for their ability to destroy myeloma cells in the bone marrow while leaving normal cells unharmed.

The breadth of research undertaken by scientists across Canada made possible by Terry's efforts is breathtaking:

- In Vancouver, at the University of British Columbia, Nelly Auersperg and her team are looking at the early genetic changes that lead to ovarian cancer and identifying which women are at high risk of developing it.
- In Toronto, at Mount Sinai Hospital, Alan Bernstein is studying genes that control the behaviour of stem cells and genetic changes that lead to leukemia. These genes play a part in many different cancers, and his investigations will help us understand the genetic causes of cancer in general.
- In Kingston, Roger Deeley and his team are studying how cancer cells become resistant to many or all of the drugs being used to destroy them.
- In Toronto, at the Hospital for Sick Children, Brenda Gallie's work with children with a rare eye cancer known as retinoblastoma has been internationally recognized. She has been successful in saving eyes that would previously been

lost. Retinoblastoma is caused by the loss of the RB gene, one of the first tumour-suppressor genes to be discovered, and Gallie is investigating why the loss of this gene causes cancer only in eye cells.

- At the Montreal Neurological Institute, Josephine Nalbantoglu and her team are studying treatments of glioma, the most common type of brain cancer, for which is there is no known cure.
- Mark Henkelman, vice-president of research at Toronto's Sunnybrook and Women's College Health Science Centre, and his team have become world leaders in the field of medical imaging, which aids in early detection, and allows doctors to see tumours better and use less invasive surgeries for their removal.

In another spinoff, one Terry Fox–funded scientist went on to found a Canadian biotechnology company. Michael Longenecker's research at the University of Alberta and collaboration with Tony Noujaïm led to the founding of Biomira Inc. in 1985. Biomira has developed a vaccine to be used against cancers of the colon, pancreas, ovary, and breast.

At Mount Sinai Hospital in Toronto, Tony Pawson says that Terry Fox funding has allowed him to build up a laboratory that has become internationally known and where post-doctoral scientists can train. He can have all the good ideas in the world, he said, but he also needs colleagues to put those ideas into practice.

Pawson has been studying how cells receive information from the outside and how they are transmitted. Once these pathways are understood, scientists may be able to design specific drugs to treat particular cancers. Chemotherapies have been useful in treating many cancers, though doctors haven't fully understood why they have been effective. That's changing now. Moreover,

Pawson's discoveries in the breakdowns in communication between cells are important in understanding other diseases such as diabetes, immunodeficiency, and neurological disorders.

"Cancer isn't a mystery any more," Pawson says. "We understand the molecular basis for the development of cancer the way scientists in the nineteenth century understood that bacteria causes disease."

Pawson, who moved to Canada in 1981, comes to mind as a leading candidate for a Nobel Prize, says Robert Phillips, executive director of the National Cancer Institute of Canada. Without Terry Fox funding, Pawson and his colleagues would likely not have been able to stay in Canada to pursue their work.

Terry may have sounded naïve when he said in 1980 that he was going to do everything he could to find a cure for cancer, but it was a great and important idea, Pawson said, not unlike John F. Kennedy's famous vow to put a man on the moon by the end of the 1960s.

"It changed the culture in which we operated," said Pawson. "Instead of some vague belief that someday, somehow, we might find more effective cures, he created an environment that said this should and could be done. I found it a powerful statement, especially coming from someone dying from the disease."

Advances in treatment and understanding of how cancer works have further increased the chances for survival for young patients with osteogenic sarcoma, the cancer Terry had, to about 70 per cent. In Terry's time, amputation controlled the disease while chemotherapy mopped up anything left behind, says Dr. David Malkin, a pediatric oncologist at the Hospital for Sick Children. Doctors today will do everything they can to avoid amputating a limb. Instead, they remove the tumour and reconstruct the tissue around it. They also give a couple of cycles of chemotherapy before surgery, which was not the practice in Terry's time. As doctors gradually develop an understanding of the biology of osteosarcoma, they can develop treatments, including new drug therapies specifically targeted to the genetic make-up of the sarcoma.

"If Terry wasn't successful in his dream to cure cancer, clearly he put the word cancer in the public's mouth," says Malkin. "It was out of the closet. I suspect before the early eighties, a kid with cancer was seen as having a death sentence. He showed that you can live with cancer, you can be productive. Part of his legacy was to show you don't go to your room and hide."

Terry's legacy went beyond inspiring cancer patients. Young people with disabilities saw that Terry never tried to hide the fact that he was running on an artificial limb.

Vancouver prosthetist Ben Speicher, who made Terry's leg, said Terry changed the way amputees used their artificial limbs. "He inspired a lot of people to get off their behind and do things. Years ago, they would have tried to hide it and not let anybody know they had one. Today, a lot of people don't even want to have a cosmetic covering on the leg. They want to show the skeleton of the leg.

"He really sticks in my mind as a turning point. After that, a lot of amputees started doing their own thing. He was the trigger for it."

Rob Snoek, an amputee sprinter and silver-medallist in the Paralympic Games, agrees. By running in a public way, Terry showed he was never ashamed of his disability. He believes Terry's demanding athleticism also led to advances in prosthetic technology. "It always bugged me people don't understand how much of an athlete Terry was to run a marathon a day on that technology. To do it with the advanced technology I have today would still be brutal."

Today, athletes are running with microprocessor-controlled prosthetic knee joints. Amputee runners have accomplished tremendous times in their sports: Earle Connor of Saskatoon, for example, is an at-the-knee amputee and holds the world record for running the hundred metres: 12.86 seconds. To give a comparison, able-bodied sprinter Maurice Greene holds the world record for the hundred metres – 9.79 seconds.

"Terry is arguably the most famous Canadian in history," says Snoek. "People around the world know him. As an amputee, it took years to understand what he meant to Canada and to me. He was willing to step out as a person with a disability and an amputee and not be ashamed. At that time I was very self-conscious, and he didn't seem to worry about that. That's the way to be."

Others agree with Snoek's observation. At the end of the twentieth century, polls and surveys were conducted to determine who were the greatest Canadians – statesmen, scientists, athletes – in history. Terry was named Canada's greatest hero, one who unified the country with his courage, in a national survey conducted by the Dominion Institute and the Council for Canadian Unity. More than twenty-eight thousand votes were logged on the institute's Web site. Frederick Banting, who discovered insulin, was ranked second, while Lester B. Pearson, who won the 1956 Nobel Peace Prize and later became prime minister, ranked third.

At the same time, on the TSN Web site there was a lively debate over the most significant Canadian sports moment of the century. Paul Henderson's winning goal against the U.S.S.R. in the 1972 Summit Series won the poll, but many argued that Terry's epic run was a far greater achievement.

Twenty years on, we talk about Terry. At dinner tables, conversation still turns to him: people remember where they saw him, how they felt. Others remember where they were when they learned that Terry had stopped running. A physiotherapist working on her patient recalls being a fifteen-year-old girl with a summer job in her father's medical practice in Brantford when she saw Terry run by. "He inspired me to do something with my life, to make a difference somehow," says Pam Honeyman. An airline ticket agent tells Fred Fox how he was a troublemaking teenager until he saw Terry run. He turned his life around. Terry had that effect on people.

Rick Hansen, who felt a kinship with Terry in many ways, watched him struggle through pain and emerge transformed. He was not a cancer victim, he was a survivor. He had taken control, made his choices, and displayed all of this on the national stage. It had a powerful effect not only on those with cancer and with disabilities, but any of us, regardless of our lot in life.

"You can choose the way you look at your life," says Hansen. "You can classify yourself as a victim and let the disease take over, or you can shape it and use it to enhance and improve your life. It's the choice Terry made. He said, 'I choose to win, to make something of my life.'"

By the time Terry started running, he had left far behind him those days when he felt humiliated to be seen without his wig. He was comfortable with himself, Hansen says. He saw himself as whole. Everyone who met Terry could see that: they didn't see disability, they saw ability. "He turned it around completely. What was perceived as a limitation became a great opportunity. People with disabilities started looking at things differently. They came away with huge pride."

Hansen says success in life isn't measured by the destination, but by the journey. After Thunder Bay, Terry's journey took on a life of its own. Terry became a great symbol of life.

We related to Terry and continue to remember him for his sense of adventure, his giving nature, and the way he cared for others. "Though he ran from St. John's to Thunder Bay, Terry's journey has truly spanned the globe," Hansen says.

On April 12, 2000, Lloyd Robertson, the respected and long-serving anchor on the CTV national news, remembered Terry's beginnings and ended his nightly broadcast with a tribute. He remembered how he and others who covered the story of Terry's death were in tears.

"What was it that made Terry so important to us?" Robertson asked. "To me he embodied the best of the Canadian spirit. We are a generous people, fair-minded, not stridently patriotic, but deeply proud of our country. And we're courageous when we have to be – just like him.

"He was our hero. He was one of us – a true-grit Canadian."

More than twenty years after he dipped his artificial leg in the Atlantic Ocean, our thoughts turn back to St. John's, where the story began with such hope and promise and, because it was so much a part of Terry, laughter.

Dorothy Wyatt is no longer the mayor of St. John's but, at age seventy, she is still serving on the city council. She recalls scanning Terry that April day with the practised eye of a former nurse. She didn't see disability either. She admired the way he was so casual and natural about his artificial leg. She remembers her playful run up the hill in pursuit of Terry. She never ran up that hill after any other runner, and there were many who followed. Over the years she met a variety of famous people, from movie stars to Queen Elizabeth, but Terry was in a category all his own. He ranks first in her memories. She visited his grave in Port Coquitlam and laid a wreath. It had been raining when she arrived, and then the sun came out. It was as if he had not left, she says.

Some say that we remain attached to Terry, that we think of him as a hero and thousands around the world follow his footsteps, because he died young, unable to conquer the disease that was trailing him as he ran Canada's highways. That's not the way at all, Wyatt said. It wasn't in his dying that he achieved his purpose.

It was in his living.

16

"I'M NOT GOING TO LOSE
EVEN IF I DIE"

"I don't care what percentages the doctor tells me I have. If God is true, I know I've got 100 per cent, if that's what He has in His plans for me. And if I really believe and if God is really there, then I'm not going to lose even if I die, because it's supposed to be the pearly gates I'm going through, and if heaven is there, I can't lose out.

"It's something I have to have a lot of faith in, and I've got to be as strong as I can and I've got to believe it. The situation I'm in right now, I could be down, I could be depressed, I could be out of it, I could be feeling sorry for myself, all of this, but I've got to have hope.

"It's all an attitude, whatever your situation in life. I could be bitter, but I can't be that way, because even if I only have two months to live I want to live those two months as best as I can, as healthy as I can, as happy as I can. I don't want to be upsetting other people by my depression. I want to help them as much as I can. I know it's hard on my parents, it's hard on my brothers. I often wonder, How is Judy doing? She goes to school, and at home her brother has a reaction and he's in bed, he's wiped out. It's probably harder on them than it is on me, because I can do something about it. I'm able to fight it, and they probably don't understand as much as I do that I can do it.

"This is where we're really talking about life. Like Doug. He phoned Rika and said, 'You know, I'm praying for Terry and he doesn't seem to be getting any better. What's going on?' When I heard that, it just made me feel great because of the thought that he was doing that for me. Now we're really talking about what's keeping me going. Through my whole run I thought about the meaning of life. I thought about so many things. I realized that wealth is nothing, because I haven't got any wealth and that didn't make any difference to me. Fame? I've become famous; it hasn't changed my life, and yet you know that's what people right now spend their whole lives striving for.

"On my run, when I got emotional, it was because I was happy, it was a life-happening, like that girl Anne Marie Von Zuben, who lost her hair three or four times in chemotherapy treatments and she was still there. She gave me a flower and, boy, that really hit me, that was a great one.

"Maybe now instead of being afraid and saying, 'Well, look how hard Terry tried and he's still got it,' people will say, 'Look at the effort he put in, and he died of cancer. We're really going to have to try hard in order to beat it, try harder than we ever have before.'"

CHRONOLOGY

July 28, 1958	Terrance Stanley Fox is born in Winnipeg, Manitoba, to Betty and Rolly Fox.
March 9, 1977	Terry's right leg is amputated six inches above the knee after cancer is discovered. He reads about an amputee runner the night before his surgery and dreams of running.
February 1979	Terry begins training for his Marathon of Hope by running one-quarter of a mile. He eventually runs 3,159 miles in training.
October 1979	In a letter to the Canadian Cancer Society, Terry asks for support for his run. "Somewhere the hurting must stop. . . . [I am] determined to take myself to the limit for this cause."
April 12, 1980	Terry begins the Marathon of Hope, his dream of running across Canada to raise money for cancer research. He dips his

	artificial leg in the harbour at St. John's, Newfoundland. His friend, Doug Alward, is his driver.
May 7, 1980	Arrives in Nova Scotia. "When I ran with the kids I really burned it to show them how fast I could go. They were tired and puffing."
May 24, 1980	Arrives in Prince Edward Island. "I was very sore and tired. It was very hard to even walk. I've got to get up and over the pain threshold."
May 27, 1980	Arrives in New Brunswick. His younger brother, Darrell, seventeen, joins the Marathon of Hope.
June 10, 1980	Arrives in Quebec. He receives little support and is repeatedly nearly run off the road.
June 28, 1980	Arrives in Ontario. Despite sweltering temperatures and crowds along the way, he continues to run the average of a marathon, twenty-six miles, a day.
September 1, 1980	Terry stops running east of Thunder Bay, Ontario. Cancer has spread to his lungs. He has run 3,339 miles in 143 days. "I felt like I had won. I felt like I had made it, even though I hadn't."
September 1980	Isadore Sharp promises that a run will be held each year in Terry's name. "We will not rest until your dream to find a cure for cancer is realized." Terry has raised $1.4 million for cancer research.
September 9, 1980	In a nationwide telethon, the CTV network raises more than ten million dollars for cancer research.

September 18, 1980 Terry is made the youngest Companion of the Order of Canada in a special ceremony in his hometown, Port Coquitlam, B.C.

October 21, 1980 The province of British Columbia honours Terry with the Order of the Dogwood.

November 22, 1980 The American Cancer Society presents Terry with its highest honour, the Sword of Hope.

December 18, 1980 Terry wins the Lou Marsh Trophy for outstanding athletic achievement.

December 23, 1980 Terry is named newsmaker of the year by Canadian Press. He wins again the following year, posthumously.

February 1981 $24.17 million has been raised. Terry's dream of getting one dollar from every Canadian is realized.

June 28, 1981 Terry dies in the Royal Columbian Hospital in New Westminster, B.C., one month before his twenty-third birthday.

July 17, 1981 A 2,639-metre peak in the Selwyn Range of the Rocky Mountains is named Mount Terry Fox.

July 30, 1981 A fifty-mile section of the Trans-Canada highway between Nipigon and Thunder Bay is named the Terry Fox Courage Highway.

August 29, 1981 Terry is posthumously inducted into the Sports Hall of Fame.

September 13, 1981 In the first Terry Fox Run, 300,000 take part and raise $3.5 million.

September 1990 More than one million people take part in the Terry Fox Run and raise $7.2 million.

December 1990 Terry is named Athlete of the Decade by The Sports Network (TSN).

| June 30, 1999 | Terry is named Canada's greatest hero in a national survey by the Dominion Institute and the Council for Canadian Unity. |
| September 1999 | About 1.5 million people in Canada and around the world take part in the Terry Fox Run and raise $17.9 million. Of that, $5.5 million is raised in international runs. |